CHRISTIANITY E✝PLORED

THE ULTIMATE DISCOVERY

paternoster
Lifestyle

First published in 2001 by Paternoster Lifestyle

Reprinted 2001, 2002

Paternoster Lifestyle is an imprint of Paternoster Publishing,
PO Box 300, Carlisle, Cumbria, CA3 0QS, UK
And PO Box 1047, Waynesboro, GA 30830-2047, USA
www.paternoster-publishing.com

British Library Cataloguing in Publication Data
A catalogue record for this book is available from the British Library

ISBN 1-85078-380-2

Designed by Diane Bainbridge
Printed in Great Britain by Bell and Bain, Glasgow

RICO TICE — THE AUTHOR

Rico Tice has been curate with responsibility for evangelism at *All Souls Church*, Langham Place, London, since 1994. He read history at Bristol University, and was at theological college at Wycliffe Hall, Oxford. He has spent time working for churches in the inner city of Liverpool and Bristol, as well as serving as a Lay Assistant at Christ Church Clifton, Bristol. Prior to ordination, he worked in training and development at Hewlett Packard. A former captain of the Bristol University Rugby Team, his hobbies also include reading and golf.

WE'RE MORE WICKED THAN WE EVER REALISED

BUT MORE LOVED

THAN WE EVER DREAMED

THE ACKNOWLEDGMENTS

Anything that we have achieved has been achieved as a team and therefore thanks are due to Richard Bewes and the All Souls Church staff for all their support. Particularly, my thanks go to the Steering Committee: Ian Roberts, Richard Trist and Elrose Hunter for their wisdom and planning, to Rosemary Jubraj for her tireless efficiency and calm demeanour, and to Jeremy Thomas and others, without whose support this project would not have been possible.

I would like to thank the editor, Carol Grugeon, for the professionalism, commitment and expertise which she brought to this guide.

I would like to acknowledge the influence of the Australian clergyman, Michael Bennett, on an earlier course run at All Souls Church called *Christianity Explained*. Thanks, too, to Tim Thornborough of the Good Book Company who brought *Christianity Explained* to England, and to Chris Hobbs, curate of All Souls Church from 1991 to 1995 for laying the foundations of so much of what we do.

Other churches and organisations have obviously been a great help to us and I would particularly like to thank Andrew Baughen of St James, Clerkenwell for the Sports Stadium evangelism concept. Thanks, too, to Holy Trinity Brompton and Willow Creek Church, Chicago, who in many ways provided the model for how to do the work of evangelism in big cities. Thanks to UCCF for all their advice in helping think through how to present this material. I am also grateful to Michael You, Paul Clark and Mark O'Donoghue of St Helen's Bishopsgate for all their help with teaching Mark's Gospel - particular thanks to Mark, who wrote much of the Bible study material. Also, to the hundreds of course participants who have filled out questionnaires and the many leaders who have written in with suggestions, my heartfelt thanks.

Lastly, to the two men who led me to Christ, Christopher Ash, and my brother, George: I am forever in your debt.

Rico Tice,
All Souls Church, Langham Place, London

CHRISTIANITY
EXPLORED

Four components of the *Christianity Explored* material are available and dovetail together to provide a comprehensive resource:

 contains all the training material for the group leaders, the teaching material for the course and practical information on how to get started. Copies of all the resource material required week-by-week is included here, including paper copies of illustrations and talk headings to be photocopied onto transparencies, as well as handouts to be photocopied for distribution. Each church running *Christianity Explored* should have one Handbook for the overall course leader to work through.

 contains all the training material for leaders, in addition to the study material given to course participants, with suggested answers, key points from each passage and examples of anticipated points of difficulty. Each group leader taking part in *Christianity Explored* should have this Guide.

 contains a brief introduction to the course, some notes on reading Mark's Gospel, summaries of the talks and study guides to work through week by week. Churches will need to purchase sufficient quantities to give one to each participant as they join the course.

 of the talks - these are available as a box set. Feedback from other leaders has suggested that listening to the tapes has brought the written course material 'alive'. We would recommend that the overall course leader listens to them before giving the talks. The tapes are not intended to replace a 'live' speaker.

1 - INTRODUCTION

Overview of the three foundations at the heart of Christianity Explored: the Bible, grace and relationships.

2 - STRUCTURE OF THE COURSE

Breakdown of the three teaching divisions: Christianity is Christ, What is the Christian life like? and Choosing to follow Christ.

3 - MOTIVATING THE CHURCH FAMILY

Teaching material to motivate and mobilise the church family in evangelism.

4 - LEADERS TRAINING NOTES

Talk outlines for the two Group Leader training sessions that group leaders attend, including detailed information on how each week of Christianity Explored is put together and training material on how to communicate the gospel. There is also a section on suggested means of follow up once the course has finished.

THE LEADER'S GUIDE

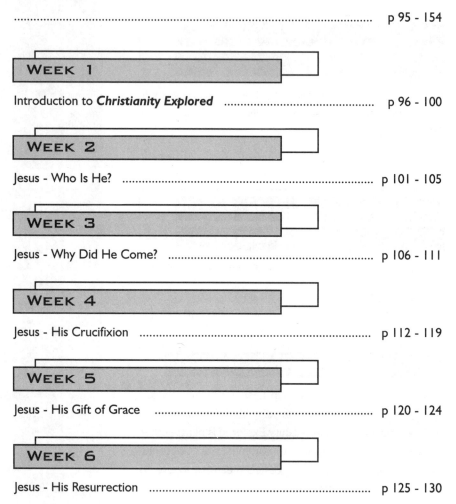

5 - STUDY GUIDES

Bible studies for course participants, which include a summary of each talk and questions on the relevant passage. Additional notes for the leaders on the answers, key points of the passage and possible points of difficulty that participants may raise are also included.

CHRISTIANITY
EXPLORED

WEEKEND/DAY AWAY

WEEK 7

WEEK 8

WEEK 9

WEEK 10

APPENDICES

Recent statistics show that 88% of the population seldom, if ever, go to church. That's a heart-rending figure if you believe that a person's ultimate success or failure in life depends on their response to Jesus Christ. However, it is a clear reflection of the erosion of our Christian inheritance and our current lamentable understanding of who Jesus is, why he came, and what it means to follow him. Sadly, this also seems to be the case even among many regular churchgoers.

Christianity Explored is an evangelistic course for committed Christians to use as a tool to reach their unbelieving friends, colleagues and family. A ten-week course based on talks, Bible study and group discussion, it aims to introduce people to the person of Jesus Christ, through Mark's Gospel, in an environment where they are free to ask any question.

Like so many churches, **All Souls Church has wrestled with how best to communicate the unchanging gospel of Jesus Christ in a changing world**, and this material has been developed over the past nine years within the context of this large international church in the centre of London. However, it is a resource designed to serve you and the people you seek to reach and is not intended to be an inflexible and prescriptive monolith. You may need to adapt the material for your own context, using illustrations and personal anecdotes to which your course participants can relate.

THE
UNCHANGING GOSPEL
OF JESUS CHRIST
IN A CHANGING WORLD

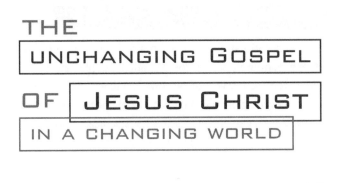

Whatever your situation, however, there are **three rock solid foundations** which are fundamental to the course:

1 THE BIBLE

- LET THE GOSPEL TELL THE GOSPEL

In his book, *Evangelicalism in Britain 1935-1995*, Oliver Barclay concluded: 'The greatest threat to evangelical strength comes if we slip into a superficiality of biblical input and fail to address the relative biblical illiteracy of our generation.'

Christianity Explored seeks to meet that threat head on by putting the Bible, and more specifically Mark's Gospel, into the hands of enquirers from Week 1. We seek to teach Christ as he walks off the pages of Mark's Gospel, grounding each journey to faith in biblical truths that are not only taught but self-discovered. Teaching Christ through Mark's Gospel is, therefore, right at the heart of the course.

2 GRACE

A firm and counter-cultural emphasis on sin makes *Christianity Explored* a disturbing experience. The problem of sin is outlined in different ways throughout the course to provide an honest portrayal of the human condition and to fully teach the wonder of grace. **Grace is only amazing when sin is seen clearly** and it is a central precept that grasping an understanding of grace will not only empower the Christian life but create a tremendous sense of joy and thanksgiving. This strategy relies strongly on prayer that the participants will be convicted of their sin, in addition to the honesty and compassion of the leaders.

3 RELATIONSHIPS

We live in a lonely culture and **a central aim of the course is that people not only make friends, but are genuinely cared for**. Whether people respond to Christ or not, we should model something of his love to them, with leaders prepared not just to give up an evening of their time each week, but to share their lives. Experience at All Souls Church has shown that this has significant impact and leads to lasting friendships which come out of authentic relationships. On previous courses leaders have invited their groups on holiday, become flatmates with participants - or even married them! The Weekend or Day Away is, therefore, an integral element. It provides an opportunity to take time out and reflect on important issues, allowing participants to count the cost of becoming a Christian and also giving them an experience of how committed Christians live together. It is noticeable that those participants who come on the Weekend Away are more likely to remain part of the church. They have spent some quality time and got to know people at a deeper level than is possible in the distracted rush of a mid-week get-together. As one participant commented, 'When I went away on a weekend, it was like seeing things go from black and white to colour.'

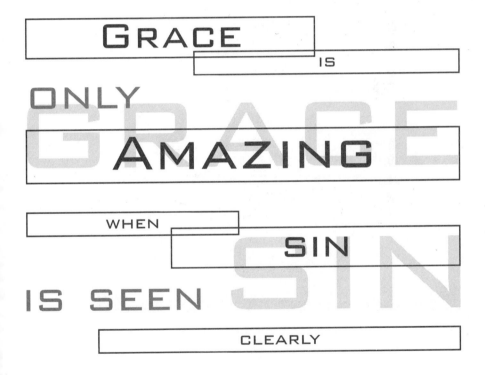

GRACE IS ONLY AMAZING WHEN SIN IS SEEN CLEARLY

Christianity Explored **introduces people to the person of Christ as he walks off the pages of Mark's Gospel**, and provides the information they need to choose to follow Christ in the life of 'obedience that comes from faith' (Rom. 1:5).

Split broadly into three sections, it allows participants to discover what Christianity is, what the Christian life is like, and what it means to choose to follow Christ.

WEEKS 1-6:

CHRISTIANITY IS CHRIST

The course begins with an emphasis on **listening**. While there is a short introduction to the first session, we are really seeking to understand why people have come and what their big issues are: discovering and exploring together is central to the whole of the course. **If we listen to people in Week 1, and hear what they have to say, they are more likely to come back**.

The following five weeks focus on the reality of Christ, as we read and teach Mark's Gospel. In particular, they draw out the problem of sin and the wonder of forgiveness. Participants discover that Christianity is about knowing Jesus personally and being known by him, rather than focusing on going to church or following rules.

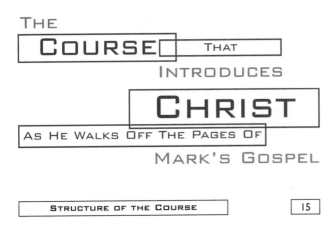

THE
COURSE THAT
INTRODUCES
CHRIST
AS HE WALKS OFF THE PAGES OF
MARK'S GOSPEL

STRUCTURE OF THE COURSE

WEEKEND OR DAY AWAY:

WHAT IS THE CHRISTIAN LIFE LIKE?

The Weekend or Day Away should show people realistically what the Christian life is like and reassure them that they are not alone as they face the battles that lie ahead. As these battles are outlined, participants are given the choice to count the cost and are assured that God has graciously given us his church family, his Holy Spirit, prayer and the Bible to uphold us.

This event falls between Weeks 6 and 7 of the course and is deliberately planned between the preceding talks on grace and the final section which invites participants to repent and believe: it is important that people have a clear understanding of the truth of the Christian life before committing to it (2 Cor. 4:2).

During this time we also seek to model something of the joy of Christian friendship. While a weekend obviously provides more time together it is not always practical or appropriate and a Saturday event can work well too.

Those who have not yet professed faith should be made to feel absolutely at home and because of that there should be no corporate singing, praying or spiritual intensity which could make participants feel pressurised or uncomfortable.

WEEKS 7-10: CHOOSING TO FOLLOW CHRIST

At the end of Week 7, and again at the end of Week 10, we give people the opportunity to receive Christ as their master and their Saviour; to choose to follow Christ by praying a prayer of commitment This part of the course is focused on appealing to the will of the participant. What choices will they make?

Our objective in these final weeks is therefore to continually emphasise Christ's call to take up their cross and follow him (Mk. 8:34). The challenge of what it means to follow Jesus and what it means to turn our back on him is highlighted in Weeks 7, 9 and 10 with talks from Mark's Gospel based on the lives of Peter and the disciples; Herod; James, John and Bartimaeus. The accompanying Bible studies also help the participants wrestle with this theme.

The topic of assurance in Week 8 is directed at those who have professed faith. It explains the devil's desire to attack their new relationship with Christ and lays the foundation of that relationship in the cross, the Bible and the Spirit's work.

Overview of Christianity Explored

Talks	Bible Studies

Weeks 1-6
Christianity is Christ

Talks	Bible Studies
Introduction	Mark 1:1-Mark 3:6
Jesus – Who is He?	Mark 3:7-Mark 5:43
Jesus – Why Did He Come?	Mark 6:1-Mark 8:30
Jesus – His Crucifixion	Mark 8:31-Mark 10:52
Jesus – His Gift of Grace	Mark 11:1-Mark 13:37
Jesus – His Resurrection	Mark 14:1-Mark 16:8

Weekend/Day Away
What is the Christian Life Like?

Talks	Bible Studies
You're Never Alone – the Church Family	
You're Never Alone – the Holy Spirit	John 14:15-18
You're Never Alone – Prayer	
You're Never Alone – the Bible	
The Motivation to Keep Going	Ephesians 2:8-9

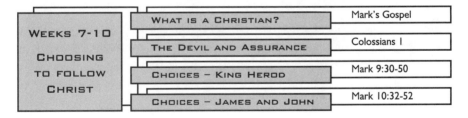

Weeks 7-10
Choosing to follow Christ

Talks	Bible Studies
What is a Christian?	Mark's Gospel
The Devil and Assurance	Colossians 1
Choices – King Herod	Mark 9:30-50
Choices – James and John	Mark 10:32-52

There are two essentials to the successful running of the course:

- **Your church family should have confidence in the course material and in the leaders.**

This can be developed through the testimonies of people who have come to faith through the course, and by encouraging as many as possible to become involved in the leadership and organisation. It is also important to ensure that the church family understands the three course foundations - the Bible, grace and relationships - and prays regularly about the course in church prayer meetings.

- **They should be motivated to invite and bring their unbelieving friends.**

In this chapter we will consider why the church family should be mobilised in evangelism and suggest some practical applications

WHY EVANGELISE?

A church family motivated to evangelise:

1 really understands how much people matter to God;

2 is committed to the Gospel and has a clear understanding of the reality of heaven and hell;

3 recognises that everyone has a role in evangelism.

PEOPLE MATTER TO GOD

1 PEOPLE MATTER TO GOD (Lk. 15:1-32)

WE ARE LOST

We have lost contact with the shepherd - we are like sheep that are lost.

WE MATTER

In all three parables that Jesus tells in Luke 15:1-32, something which is of great value to someone goes missing - a sheep, a coin, a son. Jesus is illustrating the extent to which people who are lost matter to the Father. On each occasion in the parables an *all-out* search is made for the lost item. The shepherd goes after the sheep until he finds it (v. 4); the woman sweeps the house and searches carefully until she finds the coin (v. 8); the father's eyes are scanning the horizon for his son (v. 20). We matter so much to God that he sent his Son, our shepherd, to search us out and do whatever it takes to bring us back to the Father - even dying on a cross.

THERE'S A CELEBRATION

Jesus tells us that finding what was lost merits great celebration. If you have ever lost something precious to you - your Filofax, phone, or even your parents in a shop when you were a child - the sense of relief and joy to be reunited is enormous. Verse 7 tells me that there was rejoicing right across heaven on the day that I came home to my Father. This is emphasised further in verse 10: there is a party in heaven when one person repents.

We never lock eyes with someone who does not matter to God, who does not warrant an all-out search and for whom the whole of heaven would not rejoice if they were to bow down and confess Christ as Lord.

2 HELL IS REAL (Lk. 16:19-31)

Jesus is the most tender-hearted man that ever lived, yet here he warns us of the destiny of a man who ignored the warnings of Scripture.

HELL IS A PLACE (V. 23)

To say there is no hell is to call Jesus a liar. How can we believe what he tells us about heaven if we don't believe what he tells us about hell?

HELL IS A PLACE OF SUFFERING (V. 24)

'I am in agony in this fire.' God will not have his character violated in his world and pretend it doesn't matter. Every sin must be paid for. Here we are taught that those who choose to ignore God and pay for their sin themselves will endure conscious agony after death.

HELL IS A PLACE OF SEPARATION (V. 26)

The words 'too late' are written over the gates of hell (Heb. 9:27). Once we have died we face God at the judgement and we either pay for our sin ourselves in hell or, having trusted Christ, have the joy of knowing Jesus has paid the price for us. God is a just God; and hell is where the lost are heading if they continue to accept God's gifts but ignore the giver, as this man does in verse 25. The reality of hell, and the fact that the lost will be eternally separated from God and from us, should motivate us all. Indeed, it should lead us to tears, in the way Paul weeps for his people in Romans 9 and Jeremiah mourns for people in Jeremiah 20. Have you ever wept at the fate of the lost? It's a biblical response.

Having heard this chilling parable from the Lord Jesus, we need to ask ourselves two questions:

1 Do we believe it?

2 Do we love people?

If we do, then friendships with unbelievers will take priority in the diary and will compel us to make time to pray that their eyes will be opened to their need of rescue.

3 EVERYONE HAS A ROLE IN EVANGELISM

Everyone, from the committed Christian to the unbeliever, seems to have an image of what an 'evangelist' is like. Test this out by asking your church family the following questions:

• What words describe your image of an evangelist?

• Name one person who had a strong influence upon you becoming a Christian.

• What words describe this person and their **attitude** towards you?

• How did they make you **feel**?

• What did they **say** that made a difference to you?

• What did they **do** that made a difference?

The contrast between our stereotypical image of an evangelist and the actual person who influenced us is likely to be fairly strong:

WORDS OFTEN USED TO DESCRIBE OUR IMAGE OF AN EVANGELIST
• Bible basher • Street preacher • Fanatic • Fundamentalist • Arrogant • Intimidating • TV evangelist • Brainwashing • Insensitive

WORDS OFTEN USED TO DESCRIBE THE PERSON WHO HAD A STRONG INFLUENCE UPON OUR BECOMING A CHRISTIAN
• Gentle • Patient • Passionate • Sincere • Hospitable • Genuine • Concerned • Generous • Loving • Truthful • Consistent • Humble • Forthright • Available • Self-sacrificing with time

Satan has sold us a lie about evangelists. As a result, most of us have failed to share our faith in Christ at times, either through embarrassment or because we did not think we had what it took. The fact is that most of us came to Christ through Christians who are 'normal'.

Likewise, being an evangelist or a witness for Christ does not mean you need to be another Billy Graham: you simply need to be **yourself as a Christian**. God made us who we are (Ps. 139:13-16) and he does not make mistakes. We do have what it takes; we just have to be ourselves and find the style which suits our personality. The New Testament model shows us a variety of styles of witness, and ours may be one or several of the following:

• Confrontational, e.g. Peter (Acts 2:1-39)

• Intellectual, e.g. Paul (Acts 17:16-31)

• Testimonial, e.g. the blind man (Jn. 9:1-34)

• Invitational, e.g. the woman at the well (Jn. 4:28-30)

• Serving, e.g. Dorcas (Acts 9:36)

• Interpersonal, e.g. Matthew (Lk. 5:29)

Specific material which has been developed by Willow Creek Resources to help individuals identify their personal style in evangelism can be found in Appendix 1.

CHRISTIANITY
E┼PLORED

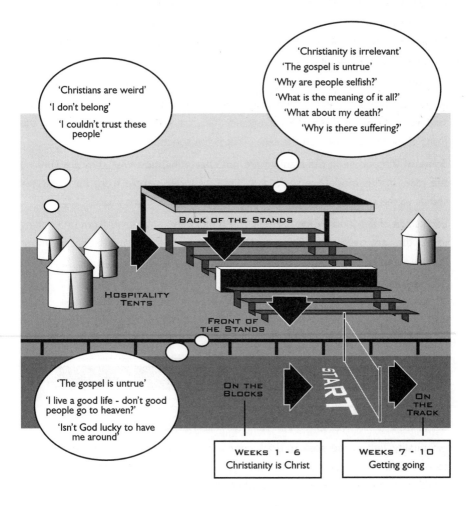

How Do We Evangelise?

Inviting Participants

Some participants may respond to the first invitation they receive and come along to the course. Alternatively, it may take months or even years of working towards this point. It is calculated that it takes an average of 32 encounters, such as chats, outreach services or challenges by friends, before someone comes to Christ. It is therefore important to prepare the church family for this to ensure that they don't become discouraged and stop trying to win their friends and family to faith.

We have found it helpful to train our church family to think of the process in terms of a **journey**, using the metaphor of a major sporting stadium event. (See page 23.)

As guests, they arrive in the hospitality tent and make their way from there to the stadium, entering at the back of the stands. Gradually, they make their way to the front of the stands to watch the race. That is the spectator's role.

Some of the people in the stadium are not spectating, however, they are running the race. In this model we seek, over time, to move people from the spectator stands to the starting blocks, ready to actually run the Christian race.

Each stage of the journey has barriers which block the unbeliever from proceeding unless they are overcome. Three of the great barriers to hearing the gospel in our culture seem to be:

- Christians are weird
- Christianity is irrelevant
- The gospel is untrue

Sports Stadium

Hospitality Tent

Hospitality Tent events seek to draw people into relationships which expose them to committed Christians who are not 'weird'. These are **relational** experiences, and the priority at these events should be to look after your guests. They are not just being brought to a talk - they are part of a whole event. People almost always need to belong before they will believe.

CHRISTIANITY
E✝PLORED

We have found that there are three vital ingredients in running these events:

- **Prayer**
- **Passion** - people, whether individually or in house groups, can run events around activities they love, such as sport, theatre, music, dance lessons, eating out, etc. Brainstorm ideas for relational activities and events which could take place in your local area, and organise a trip to a place with historic significance, a visit to an art gallery or a scenic walk.
- **Permission to fail** - if an event does not go well, never point the finger: always celebrate the fact that people have had a go. **The only sin is not to try**.

Remember that the purpose of the Hospitality Tent event is to encourage unbelievers to get to know committed Christians, so there should only be a short talk aimed at prompting questions about the Christian faith in their minds. At All Souls Church we always try to make the focus of the talk the person of Jesus, because he is so magnetic. The talk should conclude with an invitation to come to a guest service or to *Christianity Explored* to find out more - not an invitation to make a commitment to Jesus Christ.

When inviting people to *Christianity Explored* it is important to be honest about the fact that they will be offered an opportunity to explore the gospel. If people know what they are coming to, they are much more likely to stay with the course when they arrive.

Back of the Stands

These events are designed to reveal the fact that **Christianity has some very real truths to teach about issues which are relevant to us all**, such as death, meaning of life, marriage, selfishness, stress and ambition. We will, therefore, often ask Christians to speak about these at an event with a meal. Examples have included:

- A business dinner, where a senior Shell executive spoke about ambition and how he viewed that as a Christian;
- Christians in Sport events, which show that the Christian faith has the answer to growing old, getting injured and getting dropped, which sport cannot provide;
- A talk on the history of London - Twenty Centuries in Twenty Minutes - which also highlighted the Christian history of London;
- Carol Services.

These events encourage enquirers to come to **Christianity Explored** and discover more about the fundamentals of the Christian faith. Having presented Jesus Christ as the ultimate answer to these issues, we ask people to come back and investigate him further. We tell them that the heart of what we are discussing is the person of Jesus and encourage them to come and have a closer look.

FRONT OF THE STANDS

These are guest services within the church which seek to proclaim the truth and the urgency of Christ's claims. Once people have been drawn onto the fringe of our church life and begin to know that they can trust us and belong among us, we can impress upon them the claims of Christ and their very real need of forgiveness. As they hear these truths, we pray that they will commit time to coming to **Christianity Explored**, i.e. moving 'Onto the Blocks', to have a closer look at the race itself.

It may be helpful to plan events in your church around a similar structure. At All Souls Church there is a clearly structured church year, which helps the church family plan and pray about events and appropriate invitations:

SPRING

Mid January: guest events and guest services

Late January: **Christianity Explored** begins

The Spring course should be finished before Easter to avoid interrupting the weekly pattern of meeting together, so plans for a Spring course should be well underway before Christmas.

SUMMER

Early May: guest events and guest services

Mid May: **Christianity Explored** begins

AUTUMN

Early October: guest events and guest services

Mid October: **Christianity Explored** begins

All Souls Church also runs evangelism training courses for the church family two or three times a year and tries to include a couple of evangelism training sessions for house groups. These are based around a Bible passage, such as 2 Corinthians 4:1-6, where they can explore God's part and our part in evangelism.

A series of 'Hospitality Tent', 'Back of the Stands' and 'Front of the Stands' events in the one or two weeks leading up to the course, particularly using testimonies from people who have been converted at *Christianity Explored*, also inspires the church family to bring their friends along. It is a compelling reminder to even the most cynical that **the gospel changes lives**.

In addition, whenever an evangelistic application emerges from the sermon, the preacher is trained to invite any unbelievers to fill out a contact card and indicate their interest in coming to *Christianity Explored*. Strategically-placed contact cards and pens throughout the church, with collection boxes at the doors, makes this a straightforward and non-threatening process. They are then telephoned the week before the course begins, reminded that they filled out a card and invited to attend. The response to a personal phone call inviting them to supper at *Christianity Explored* is significantly higher than the response to a letter.

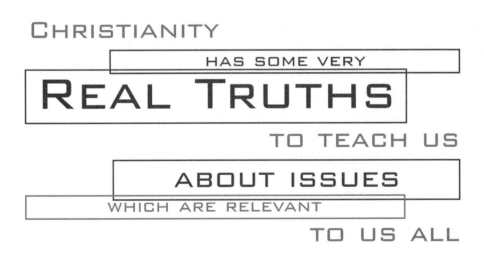

CHRISTIANITY

HAS SOME VERY

REAL TRUTHS

TO TEACH US

ABOUT ISSUES

WHICH ARE RELEVANT

TO US ALL

TRAINING SESSION 1:
ESSENTIALS OF EVANGELISM

Talk 1:   Evangelism - God's part and our part
          (15 minutes)

Talk 2:   What is it like to lead on Christianity
          Explored? (40 minutes)
          Prayer Time (20 minutes)

Talk 3:   The message and how to communicate
          it (30 minutes)

TRAINING SESSION 2:
TEACHING MARK'S GOSPEL

Talk 1:   Warnings from the parable of the sower
          (Mk. 4) (25 minutes)
          Discussion of Personal Study
          (25 minutes)

Talk 2:   Key themes in Mark's Gospel
          (25 minutes)

The talks for these sessions are given in this chapter, along with the following additional training material for reference:

• The Structure of Mark's Gospel - a summary;

• Meeting Christ in Mark - a detailed commentary;

• Frequently Asked Questions from Mark's Gospel;

• Guidelines on leading Bible studies;

• Follow Up.

LEADERS' TRAINING NOTES

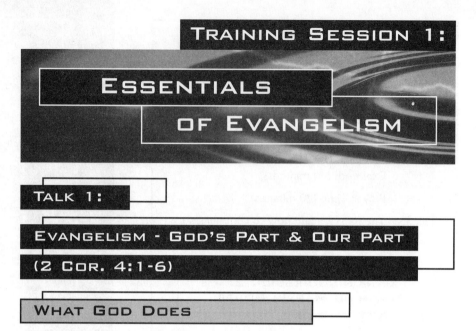

ESSENTIALS
OF EVANGELISM

TALK 1:

EVANGELISM - GOD'S PART & OUR PART
(2 COR. 4:1-6)

WHAT GOD DOES

We need to try and isolate God's part in evangelism. If we try to do God's part we'll see that it's going to be very frustrating - you have to be the creator of the universe to pull off God's part!

We're told half way through verse 6 he makes 'his light shine in our hearts to give us the light of the knowledge of the glory of God in the face of Christ' - God allows us to understand that Jesus is God and he shines the light of that knowledge into our hearts. The moment of illumination, when God, by his Holy Spirit, shines into the human heart, is a moment of identification. It's the moment when a person sees who Jesus really is. So conversion is a recognition of Jesus. When Paul is converted on the Damascus Road, he asks, 'Who are you Lord?' and is told, 'I am Jesus.' (Acts 9:5) That is the moment of his conversion, when he recognises for the first time who Jesus actually is.

God is described as the God who said, 'Let light shine out of darkness.' That is a reference to Genesis chapter 1 (Gen. 1:3) and to the miracle of creation. So, this is the God who thundered the universe into being. He speaks the universe into being by saying, 'Let there be light.' **This God who created everything now recreates the minds and hearts of people**. So God shines into the hearts and minds of people the knowledge that his son Jesus is God. This means that for anyone to become a Christian it's never just a matter of telling them the gospel - for someone to become a Christian God must, by his Holy Spirit, shine the truth of the gospel into people's minds. It is a miracle that is required, not a methodology. In other words, God performs a miracle of re-creation in our hearts, in order *to get us* to recognise that Jesus is God.

WHY PEOPLE CANNOT SEE IT

'The god of this age has blinded the minds of unbelievers ...' (v. 4)

The curtain is drawn back to reveal a supernatural battle field - we realise that it is not a case of someone simply accepting or rejecting Christ. The devil is at work preventing people recognising Jesus. He has blinded their minds (v. 4).

The phrase 'the god of this age' is a contradiction in terms. Divinity is not confined to this world - by definition it must be eternal. Clearly the 'god of this age' is no god at all, but there is a spirit at work in this age, who many serve as though he were indeed God. His aim is to make the things of this world and of this age our god, and to blind men and women to any other world and to any other age. One commentator put it like this: 'It is an idolatrous preoccupation with the material things of this passing world which renders the spiritual things of the next world undetectable to men's gaze.'

You talk to people about the things of the Spirit and of Christ and sometimes they're absolutely blind to them. Their concerns are totally contained within the here and now: the career, the family, the house, the relationship, the essay. There is a complete inability to see that there might be anything beyond that.

But the Christian who has had his or her eyes opened fixes their eyes not on what is seen but on what is unseen (2 Cor. 4:18). What is seen is temporary but what is unseen is eternal. These blind people can only see Jesus in the here and now, perhaps as a great moral teacher or just as a swear word: his eternal significance is completely lost to them. And what is Satan determined to prevent? (v. 4) That they see 'the light of the gospel of the glory of Christ, who is the image of God'. Satan is determined to prevent people recognising Jesus. That's what he has got to stop because that is **what the gospel is** - it's an **identification of Jesus**.

The two applications of these truths:

1 Gratitude

The only difference between a believer and an unbeliever is that God, in his mercy, has opened the believer's blind eyes and illuminated their heart by his Holy Spirit. As Billy Graham says, 'Conversion is the greatest miracle.' We should be forever grateful.

2 Prayer

We should pray God would open the eyes of my friends and colleagues and loved ones. As Eric Alexander states, 'Prayer is the primary evangelistic method.'

All this means that as we come to *Christianity Explored* we must remember that it is up to God whether somebody becomes a Christian or not. Only he can open blind eyes and we must trust him for the results.

SO WHAT DO WE DO?

'we... preach Jesus Christ as Lord, and ourselves as your servants for Jesus' sake.' (v. 5)

Our job is to tell people the gospel and leave the Spirit of God to convict them of its truth. The word 'preach' can evoke images of ranting clergy, but the original root word is that of a herald, someone who brings important announcements from the king to his kingdom. Heralds bring news of the king.

With regard to our manner as we bring the message, we are to be as servants for Jesus' sake (v. 5). In the Greek the word for servant literally means slave. We are to be the slaves of those to whom we bring the message. Paul was determined to present Christ to others with no hint of self promotion. These words were undoubtedly aimed at the new ministers in Corinth, whose preaching apparently focused on themselves and had the effect of making the Corinthians serve them! Calvin has commented: 'He that would preach Christ alone must of necessity forget himself.' That is a great challenge in the me-centred culture of today.

We keep telling people about the Lord Jesus and, as we do so, we pray that God will open their blind eyes.

'We do not use deception, nor do we distort the word of God ... by setting forth the truth plainly we commend ourselves to every man's conscience in the sight of God.' (v. 2)

In telling people about Christ, we use:

- **integrity - we do not use deception.**
  We are straight with people. The Corinthian false teachers promised tantalising mystical experiences for a fee. They had techniques which drew people in. But Paul says, 'No. Just preach Jesus.'

- **fidelity - we do not distort the word of God.**
  We have to tell people the tough bits. For example, that sin is a real problem, that there is a place called hell and that repentance is a necessity. In order to tell people these things we will have to believe in the work of the Holy Spirit to draw them to Christ, as we speak these hard truths.

- **intelligibility - we set forth the truth plainly.**
  We must always ask the question, 'Was that clear. Were people able to understand?'

- **humility - 'We do not preach ourselves, but Jesus Christ as Lord.' (v. 5)**
  We are to draw people to Jesus, not to us; the spotlight is on him.

SET FORTH
THE TRUTH
PLAINLY

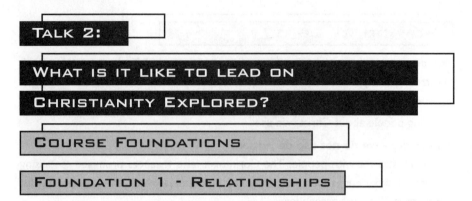

TALK 2:

WHAT IS IT LIKE TO LEAD ON CHRISTIANITY EXPLORED?

COURSE FOUNDATIONS

FOUNDATION 1 - RELATIONSHIPS

Our vision for the course is that people come to the 'obedience that comes from faith' (Rom. 1:5). Obviously, for this miracle to take place we need the Holy Spirit to open blind eyes, but we also need strong relationships in place to support those who are counting the cost of repentance. The participants must feel that:

• they belong;

• they can trust us.

It is striking that Paul was only in Thessalonica for three weeks and yet he wrote, 'We loved you so much that we were delighted to share with you not only the gospel of God but our lives as well' (1 Thes. 2:8). In a short time, Paul could reflect upon the fact that strong relationships had been formed.

One woman who came to **Christianity Explored** in 1998, and who has still not become a Christian, wrote in a letter after the course: 'The time that I spent at All Souls Church has had a profound impact on me that I struggle with daily. Undoubtedly, the single most impressive aspect has been the people - everyone I have met through **Christianity Explored** has touched me and moved me with their compassion, intelligence, commitment and sense of peace, not to mention their patience and tolerance in the face of my tirades of scepticism and anger which must have been exhausting, frustrating and seemingly endless.'

CHRISTIANITY
E✝PLORED

The evening is, therefore, structured relationally as follows:

6.30 P.M. **LEADERS' PRAYER MEETING**

- **PRAYING FOR EACH OTHER** (in their groups)
  - 10 minutes

- **SHORT TALK**
  (preparing the leaders for that evening's teaching)
  - 6 minutes

- **PRAYER FOR PARTICIPANTS** -12 minutes

7.00 P.M. | **MEAL** |

7.45 P.M. **GROUP DISCUSSION ON LAST WEEK'S STUDY**
(using the 'Big Picture' and 'Focus In' Bible study
material, as required)

8.05 P.M. | **MESSAGE** | (talk)

8.30 P.M. **GROUP DISCUSSION ON TONIGHT'S TALK**
(using the Questions for Group Discussion)

9.00 P.M. | **MINGLE** | (end of formal part of evening)

LEADERS' PRAYER MEETING

We begin the leaders' prayer meeting by focusing on our care for each other. We may often have had difficult days at work or at home (indeed, there can have been spiritual attack), and we find that all benefit greatly from a time of prayer and support before focusing on the work in hand.

To that end, the leaders get together in their groups and pray for each other from 6.30 p.m. - 6.40 p.m. There is then a short talk of approximately 6-7 minutes from the Bible which focuses our minds on the topic that is to be taught in the forthcoming session.

The remainder of the meeting is spent praying for protection from spiritual attack during the evening and for blind eyes to be opened. Each participant is briefly discussed and prayed for by name.

MEAL

The leaders are then ready to welcome the participants as they begin to arrive from 7.00 p.m. It is so important to their sense of belonging that they are welcomed by name and taken through for supper. A leader who is not there to welcome their guests is basically stating, 'You are not as important as what I have just been doing.'

Over supper we try to avoid 'heavy' theological discussions. The intention is to share life - not to be spiritually intense. We need to remember that the participants have probably been treated as a 'human resource' all day and our aim, by contrast, should be to celebrate them as human beings made in the image of God. We want people to be able to relax and, above all, realise that we are interested in all of their lives, not just the spiritual aspect.

GROUP DISCUSSION ON LAST WEEK'S STUDY

The formal part of the evening begins after supper with individual group discussion on the previous week's study. The participants will have had the opportunity to study the suggested reading - **The Big Picture of Mark's Gospel** - and may have questions from this. Experience at All Souls Church has shown that sometimes participants do not have time to do the study in advance and some weeks it doesn't take long to discuss the home study even if they have. The key thing is to make sure that people don't feel uncomfortable. The **Focus In** study section has been included to overcome this and has proved a constructive way to fill the time in such circumstances. Because it is an additional study it can work well just to go through it from scratch in your group on the night. Both these studies are included to facilitate discussion and the material you choose to draw on may vary from week to week.

MESSAGE

The main 25-minute talk follows this review discussion time. Each week focuses on a new aspect of who Jesus is, why he came and what it means to follow him through the main headings:

• Weeks 1-6: *Christianity is Christ;*
• Weekend or Day Away: *What is the Christian life like?*
• Weeks 7-10: *Choosing to follow Christ.*

Like a jigsaw puzzle gradually being put together, a new piece is added each week so that participants 'learn Christ' (Eph. 4:20). The new piece of the jigsaw is then discussed in groups after the talk.

GROUP DISCUSSION ON TONIGHT'S TALK

Having listened to the talk, it is important that the participants then feel able to speak. The leader's role in the ensuing group discussion is therefore one of listener and encourager. Clearly, there are also opportunities for teaching here but it is crucial that the participants are heard. Leaders should, therefore, try to avoid speaking in the group discussion at the expense of listening to the participants. Questions are included at the end of each talk as discussion starters and to help maintain focus.

MINGLE

After 25-30 minutes, the group discussion is called to a halt and participants are directed to next week's questions in their Study Guide. Refreshments are served and the evening is formally closed. Experience has shown that it is an issue of trust to end at the agreed time. People must be able to leave when they have planned to do so, although the hope is that participants will feel they are not required to leave immediately and can stay and chat. It is now, after the input of the talk and discussions, that the most effective one-to-one conversations take place. Many will want to talk individually to their leaders, so don't underestimate the spiritual importance of being individually available to participants at this time. This is a crucial time to teach them Christ and apply him to their situation. One of the biggest reasons that people walk away from the Christian faith is because they don't feel it is relevant to their experience of real life. This is a time to demonstrate that we can bring Christian thinking to every area of life.

LIKE A
JIGSAW PUZZLE
GRADUALLY BEING PUT
TOGETHER ...

By the end of Week 7 participants will have studied all of Mark's Gospel, and the format will vary slightly in the following weeks. Instead of undertaking personal study at home, participants will work through a Bible study relevant to the topic after the talk, with additional time devoted to this. At this stage friendships have been established and participants are usually happy to use the time prior to the talk just to chat or discuss issues raised in previous weeks. The schedule for these weeks works well as follows:

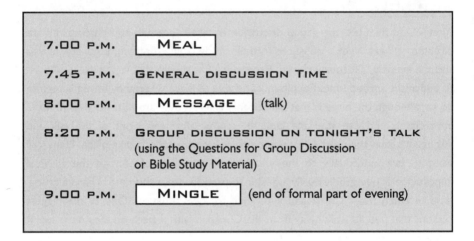

7.00 P.M.	MEAL
7.45 P.M.	GENERAL DISCUSSION TIME
8.00 P.M.	MESSAGE (talk)
8.20 P.M.	GROUP DISCUSSION ON TONIGHT'S TALK (using the Questions for Group Discussion or Bible Study Material)
9.00 P.M.	MINGLE (end of formal part of evening)

■ ■ ■ A NEW PIECE IS ADDED EACH WEEK SO THAT PARTICIPANTS 'LEARN CHRIST'

CHRISTIANITY
EXPLORED

THE WHEEL OF DISCOVERY

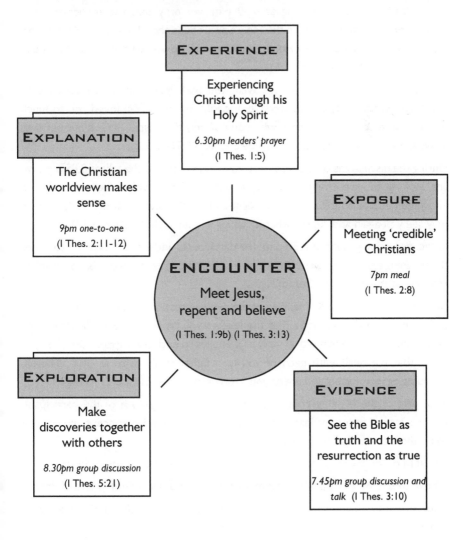

EXPERIENCE

Experiencing Christ through his Holy Spirit

6.30pm leaders' prayer
(1 Thes. 1:5)

EXPLANATION

The Christian worldview makes sense

9pm one-to-one
(1 Thes. 2:11-12)

EXPOSURE

Meeting 'credible' Christians

7pm meal
(1 Thes. 2:8)

ENCOUNTER

Meet Jesus, repent and believe

(1 Thes. 1:9b) (1 Thes. 3:13)

EXPLORATION

Make discoveries together with others

8.30pm group discussion
(1 Thes. 5:21)

EVIDENCE

See the Bible as truth and the resurrection as true

7.45pm group discussion and talk (1 Thes. 3:10)

The ultimate aim of the course is for participants to encounter Jesus, that is to recognise him as their Lord, repent and obey. As the **Wheel of Discovery** diagram on page 39 shows, the different segments of the evening are designed to facilitate that encounter. As we look at the methodology it is vital to go to Scripture. I Thessalonians gives us an insight into Paul's evangelistic method and his early ministry to young Christians. As you consider this, bear in mind that he was only in Thessalonica for three weeks (Acts 17).

In the leaders' prayer meeting at 6.30 p.m. we pray that the participants will **experience** Christ as Lord, as the Holy Spirit opens their blind eyes: 'Our gospel came to you not simply with words, but also with power, with the Holy Spirit and with deep conviction' (I Thes. 1:5).

During the meal at 7.00 p.m. we want the participants to have **exposure** to Christians, whom they see as credible, friendly and wise: 'We loved you so much that we were delighted to share with you not only the gospel of God but our lives as well, because you had become so dear to us' (I Thes. 2:8).

During the discussions of last week's study at 7.45 p.m. and the talk at 8.05 p.m. we are looking to give the participants enough *evidence* with which to make an informed decision to follow Christ: 'Night and day we pray most earnestly that we may see you again and supply what is lacking in your faith' (I Thes. 3:10).

In the discussion groups at 8.30 p.m. the participants and leaders **explore** together the meaning and relevance of the truths that have been presented: 'Test everything. Hold on to the good' (I Thes. 5:21).

At 9.00 p.m., when the formal part of the evening session finishes and people have a chance to mingle, we hope that the leaders will be able to **explain** clearly the Gospel and the Christian world view as it applies to each participant's life: 'For you know that we dealt with each of you as a father deals with his own children, encouraging, comforting and urging you to live lives worthy of God' (I Thes. 2:11-12).

Each part of the evening contributes to the Christian growth of the participant. None is more important: leaders have to see it as a cohesive concept and commit to be there from start to finish every week.

The sum of the constituent parts will lead participants to **encounter** Jesus:

• **now**, by turning 'to God from idols to serve the living and true God' (I Thes. 1:9b) and

• **for eternity**, 'blameless and holy in the presence of our God and Father when our Lord Jesus comes with all his holy ones' (I Thes. 3:13).

CHRISTIANITY
E⨯PLORED

In addition, there are three key relational 'L's for leaders:

LEARN NAMES

The sound of your name is the sweetest sound. It destroys the sense of anonymity and loneliness and makes you feel that you are known and belong. One young woman who went through the course said that it meant a great deal to her when the leader greeted her by name at the door on the second week. She felt that she belonged.

LISTEN

Week 1 begins with these questions:

• What is your name?

• Why are you here?

• **If God were here and you could ask him one question, and you knew that he would answer it, what would it be?**

This means the course begins **relationally**. We start by listening, not lecturing. When people see this they realise that we are genuinely concerned about them. Try to find out all you can about their hobbies, jobs and interests. Try to understand where they are coming from and why they are saying what they are saying. Showing care and concern is only effective if people know that it is genuine, so pray for real love for the people that you are developing relationships with.

LEAD HONESTLY

Don't pretend to have all the answers. Some questions can be easily answered but others can be very difficult. If you don't know the answer, say so - but take the trouble to get back to the person the next week with a real answer.

It is crucial that we are gracious and courteous and act as peacemakers if the discussion gets heated, making sure that each person has a chance to express their opinion. If one person's particular issue begins to dominate, gently ask him or her if you can pick that up with them at the end of the session.

The problem of sin is very clearly outlined and reinforced in the talk every week:

- In Week 2 we ask who Jesus is and see that he is a man with authority - but have we lived under his authority?

- In Week 3 we see that sin is our biggest problem and its end result is hell. We should do anything to avoid it - even cutting off a limb (Mk. 9:43-48).

- In Week 4 we see that Jesus died on the cross to pay for our sin and release us from having to pay for it ourselves in hell.

- In Week 5 we learn that grace is a gift (Eph. 2:1-10). There is nothing we can do to earn our forgiveness because our sin has put us in such debt. Like little children, we just have to receive the gift (Mk. 10:13-16).

- In Week 6 we see that the resurrection guarantees that we will be raised and judged for our sin (Acts 17:31).

- In Week 7 we learn that the Christian has much to repent of.

Throughout the course, we are praying that the participants will see the seriousness of their sin. We long for them to have a similar experience to that of Isaiah in the temple - to see God's holiness, their own uncleanness, and cry out 'Woe to me!' (Is. 6:5) As one participant wrote after she was converted: 'The Bible is a very disturbing book. It's like a mirror, and it shows us what we are really like.'

This emphasis on sin means that the groups must be 'communities of truth'. If something tough about sin is raised in one of the talks, it is usually followed by the invitation to discuss it within the groups. Adding this phrase softens the blow: it means that **we never apologise for what we say about sin but we do want to reason with people**, as Paul did in Athens (Acts 17:17). This means there needs to be a real honesty about what we are all like. Particularly in the one-to-one times, the leader's guiding principle should be 'no masks'. Often the participants find it incredibly liberating to be with people who are prepared to be honest. This can only happen because the great news of the gift of forgiveness means we are loved unconditionally. This is so liberating, not least because many have been brought up with conditional love: if I perform, if I win, then I will be loved; but if I fail, then that love will be withdrawn. Understanding that God loves me anyway is a life-changing experience. It is what J.I. Packer describes as 'the spiritual electricity that transforms the Christian life' and means that my repentance is driven not by duty but by gratitude.

Our prayer is that participants will begin to find their identity in this love, as shown by the Valjean illustration from *Les Miserables* in Week 5.

Obviously, at the heart of this teaching is utter dependence on God to open the participants' blind eyes to 'the incomparable riches of his grace' (Eph. 2:7). Our motto is, 'We're more wicked than we ever realised but more loved than we ever dreamed.' What a message!

FOUNDATION 3 - THE BIBLE

It is very striking that Jesus refuses to reveal himself to the two disciples on the Emmaus road until he has given them a Bible study. He does this because 'God's way of finding God is through the Scriptures'. We must ground people's experience of Christ in the Bible - that is where people meet the authentic Jesus.

Our aim is that the participants will leave the course having wrestled with who Jesus is, why he came and what it means to follow him. To that end we give each of them a Bible to keep at the start of the course, and we consistently focus on Mark's Gospel (the shortest!). We ask everyone to explore the truth of Mark 1:1 and find out whether this really is the great news (the gospel) about Jesus Christ, the Son of God.

So we ask participants: 'Will you please just take a Bible, read it and seek to do what it says?' And we promise that if they do they will find that it authenticates itself.

The Study Guide covers the whole of Mark's Gospel and a section is taught each week. Week 8 is the exception to this, when the talk and Bible Study is taken from Colossians 1. This is necessary to introduce the theme of Christian assurance which is vital to young believers and not covered in Mark's Gospel. A key objective of the study programme is that the participants will have grasped a real understanding of Jesus by the end of the course.

Since most people are prepared to read the Bible and test the truth of Mark 1:1, focusing discussion on the reliability of the Bible can therefore be something of a distraction. If this area is an issue for someone, however, a detailed examination of the facts is contained in the introduction of *The Study Guide*. Appendix II also contains details of the number of copies of ancient writings in existence and their age. A blank version of the table is available in *The Handbook* to use as a basis for group discussion: if you ask participants to estimate the age and dissemination of Scripture and other ancient writings, they are often surprised by the answers.

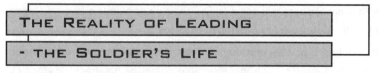

THE REALITY OF LEADING
- THE SOLDIER'S LIFE

What is it like to lead on **Christianity Explored**?

Passing on the message of the gospel is like passing the Olympic torch: you are in for a tough and gruelling time, as well as a time of joyous celebration. In Luke 15, Jesus speaks of the joy in finding the lost and describes the cosmic celebration across heaven when a sinner repents. We also feel that joy, as we are involved in the task of finding the lost.

Yet with the joy comes the reality of the task ahead. In 2 Timothy 1:8, Paul beseeches Timothy to join him in 'suffering' for the gospel. He wrote this around AD 67, chained and shackled in a Roman prison and aware that he is soon to die. Many followers of Christ have deserted him (2 Tim. 1:15) and his appeal to Timothy to join him in suffering for the gospel is not only to suffer for it, but to guard it, protect it and to pass it on.

Paul's exhortation in 2 Timothy 2:1-7, provides a good model for leaders on **Christianity Explored** - that of the dedicated soldier for whom hardship, risk and suffering are a matter of course. Soldiers do not expect an easy time. Indeed, Tertullian describes a soldier's life in this way: 'No soldier comes to the war surrounded by luxuries, nor goes into action from a comfortable bedroom, but from a makeshift and narrow tent where every kind of hardness and severity and unpleasantness is to be found.'

Being a leader on **Christianity Explored** is a hard task. It requires you to make a commitment, despite busy schedules. It also requires you to be disciplined and committed to three very important tasks:

DISCIPLINED TO STUDY

We are not required to have an answer for all the questions thrown our way during the course. We must, however, try to seek out the answer, either through searching the Bible, asking our pastor or another person, or checking out the various books and study resources available. We should never pretend to have all the answers, but we must follow up on questions and come back the following week with an answer.

COMMITTED TO SCRIPTURE

This is where the power is and it is the best tool we have. The Lord declares that his word will not return empty, but will accomplish his purpose (Is. 55:11). Again, in 2 Timothy 2:15, Paul exhorts Timothy to devote himself to the study of God's word: 'Do your best to present yourself to God as one approved, a workman who does not need to be ashamed and who correctly handles the word of truth.'

In this course it is essential to have a good knowledge of Mark's Gospel. Study it carefully and think about its application in your own life. If the Bible is living for you, it will be living for those who attend the course. You should know the structure of Mark (pages 66 and 67) so that any questions which are raised can be put in context. A working knowledge of the Study Guide for each week is also helpful, to allow you to facilitate participants who have not done the suggested reading of Mark to still grasp something of what is going on as you lead the discussion time.

COMMITTED TO SUPPLICATION

Prayer is essential before, during and after the course. There is at least some truth in John Wesley's statement that 'God has bound himself to do nothing save in answer to prayer.' However, it is also sobering to remember the warning of Isaiah 59:2, 'But your iniquities have separated you from your God; your sins have hidden his face from you, so that he will not hear.' We must understand that unrepentant sin can quench the power of our prayers. This means that my sin affects you, and your sin affects me, as we seek to proclaim the gospel together. A call to prayer is also a call to keep putting the sinful nature to death (Rom. 8:13).

Essential to all of these disciplines is **concentration**. 2 Timothy 2:4 says, 'No-one serving as a soldier gets involved in civilian affairs - he wants to please his commanding officer.' We are in the midst of a war in the weeks of this course, so we must be single-minded. The course will have a huge impact on our diaries. Time and again, as we seek to make time to lead, to prepare, to pray and to meet up with participants, the good will be enemy of the best and the urgent will be the enemy of the important. **A ruthless discipline is needed to make time to lead**.

Our enemy, Satan, hates the work we are doing. We must be prepared, through study and prayer, to take real knocks every week. We may suddenly find feelings of inadequacy or temptation creeping in. These remind us to depend on the Lord to do his work through us. Remember the athlete in 2 Timothy 2:5: 'Similarly, if anyone competes as an athlete, he does not receive the victor's crown unless he competes according to the rules.' The 'rules' for the Christian life are God's moral code laid out in Scripture. God's laws are expressions of his love for us, so we trust that our obedience will mean the best for us.

The following verse states, 'The hardworking farmer should be the first to receive a share of the crops.' Like the farmer, we must **endure** in our endeavours with those on the course. No one sees the farmer rising early and working before others are awake. For us as leaders we too face an audience of only one, i.e. the Lord Jesus. Only he will see us preparing, praying and making it here weekly. If those in our group do not make it, we keep praying. If they dismiss the Bible studies, we keep preparing. If they are late, we continue to be on time. We must not be discouraged.

This is a daunting task but the key is to remember that we are not alone and we share the work with our other group leaders. It is important to encourage one another in this task and to pray for one another to be able to balance the time pressures that face us daily and as we come together on the course.

The importance of prayer cannot be minimised as we embark on *Christianity Explored* together. Consider the example of Epaphras in Colossians. Paul says of him, 'He is always wrestling in prayer for you, that you may stand firm in all the will of God, mature and fully assured. I vouch for him that he is working hard for you and for those at Laodicea and Hierapolis' (Col. 4:12-13). We, too, need to be prepared for the hard work of prayer as we enter the battle together.

As leaders, we can share with each other the time pressures we face and how we can best pray for one another during this term of *Christianity Explored*.

We can't expect participants to be honest with us unless we begin by being honest with each other.

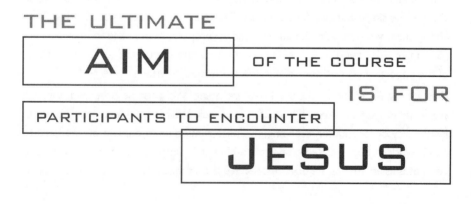

THE ULTIMATE

AIM OF THE COURSE

IS FOR

PARTICIPANTS TO ENCOUNTER

JESUS

1 LEADER NAME:	2 LEADER NAME:	3 LEADER NAME:
TIME PRESSURES:	TIME PRESSURES:	TIME PRESSURES:
SPECIFIC PRAYER POINTS:	SPECIFIC PRAYER POINTS:	SPECIFIC PRAYER POINTS:

2 WAYS TO LIVE

1

God is the loving ruler of the world.
He made the world.
He made us rulers of the world under him.

You are worthy, our Lord and God, to receive glory and honour and power, for you created all things, and by your will they were created and have their being.
Revelation 4:11

BUT IS THAT THE WAY IT IS NOW?

2

We all reject the ruler - God - by trying to run life our own way without him, but we fail to rule ourselves or society or the world.

There is no-one righteous, not even one; there is no-one who understands, no-one who seeks God. All have turned away. Romans 3:10-12

WHAT WILL GOD DO ABOUT THIS REBELLION?

3

God won't let us rebel forever.

God's punishment for rebellion is death and judgement.

Man is destined to die once, and after that to face judgement.
Hebrews 9:27

GOD'S JUSTICE SOUNDS HARD. BUT ...

4

Because of his love, God sent his son into the world: the man Jesus Christ. Jesus always lived under God's rule. Yet by dying in our place he took our punishment and brought forgiveness.

Christ died for sins once for all, the righteous for the unrighteous, to bring you to God.
1 Peter 3:18

BUT THAT'S NOT ALL ...

5

God raised Jesus to life again as the ruler of the world. Jesus has conquered death, now gives new life, and will return to judge.

In his great mercy he has given us new birth into a living hope through the resurrection of Jesus Christ from the dead. 1 Peter 1:3

WELL, WHERE DOES THAT LEAVE US?

6 THE 2 WAYS TO LIVE   A   B

A: Our way: Reject the ruler - God.
                  Try to run life our own way.
Result: Condemned by God.
                  Facing death and judgement.

B: God's new way: Submit to Jesus as our ruler.
                  Rely on Jesus' death and resurrection.
Result: Forgiven by God. Given eternal life.

Whoever believes in the Son has eternal life, but whoever rejects the Son will not see life, for God's wrath remains on him John 3:36

WHICH OF THESE REPRESENTS THE WAY YOU WANT TO LIVE?

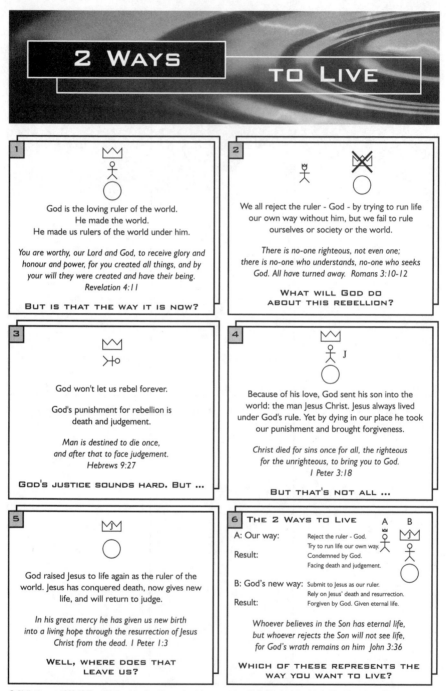

CHRISTIANITY
EXPLORED

THE MESSAGE & HOW TO COMMUNICATE IT

THE MESSAGE

Page 48 shows the **2 Ways to Live** outline. As you see, the presentation is in a logical flow of argument, with each point dependent on the one preceding it.

1 It begins with creation. This establishes God's ownership (rule) and our dependence. The relationship we have with God is that of the creature to the loving creator. **Everything we are and everything we possess comes from God**. There is no room for us to exercise independent authority or self-government.

2 Rebellion (sin) can only be understood in the light of creation. God makes us and therefore owns us. Consequently, **any attempt at self-government is a crime against our maker and owner** because we are part of his creation and are accountable to him.

If God is not creator, then sin becomes nothing more than a social disorder or psychological disease. Furthermore, understanding the consequences of sin in Genesis 3 is essential to answering questions on suffering. We live in a cursed world and as participants ask why there is suffering, we need to communicate the domino effect of mankind's sin in every area of life.

3 Once we understand our rebellion against God's ownership, judgement can be seen as the logical consequence. **God punishes us because we reject him**. The justice of God's judgement is seen when we realise how great our crime is. We have defied God's ownership of us and chosen other gods, even putting ourselves before him.

If sin is not seen as an offence against God, then judgement is unjust, or else it is reduced to the idea of natural consequences.

4 Given that God's judgement is just, we now come to his solution to our problem. God's son became a human and lived a perfect life so that he could take the punishment which humans deserve. **God sending his son to die in our place is sheer mercy**.

If we do not understand God's anger towards our sin and his rejection of us because of it, then Jesus' death does not make sense. Without judgement, the death of Jesus is emptied of purpose - it becomes at best a moral lesson and at worst a gigantic mistake.

5 **The resurrection shows that Jesus has conquered death and gives new life**. It also reveals that he will return as judge and that he is the world ruler promised by the Old Testament prophets (Acts 2:25-26).

Furthermore, we are not just saved and given new life as individuals. It was God's plan to bring all those who trust in Christ together as his family (Eph. 2:19). And so we live our resurrection life in this new family (1 Pet. 2:4-5).

6 **Faith and repentance follow from our understanding of the person and work of Jesus**. The object of our trust is Jesus because he has died to save us. The direction of our repentance is towards Jesus because he is declared to be Lord through his resurrection.

If Jesus is not Saviour and Lord, then faith is nothing more than positive thinking and repentance nothing more than a vague sense of unhappiness with ourselves.

Your personal study for this week includes learning the *2 Ways to Live* model and the appropriate verses. This framework, when mastered, is a wonderful tool which you can take with you for the rest of your lives.

HOW TO COMMUNICATE THE MESSAGE

The way we should aim to work with participants is a balance of the following:

EXPLORING

We listen very carefully to participants, to find out how they think and where they are. We keep asking ourselves, 'What is their presenting issue?' In other words, what is their headache, their big issue, the thing on their mind at the moment? It could be the death of a loved one, or the desire for a life partner, or a major disappointment. They need to know that we are engaged where they are before they will engage with us.

In his epistle, James writes, 'My dear brothers, take note of this: everyone should be quick to listen, slow to speak and slow to become angry ...' (Jas. 1:19). The need to listen is paramount, especially during Week 1 when we ask people why they are here and follow that with the big question: 'If God were here and you could ask him one question, and you knew that he would answer it, what would it be?'

CHRISTIANITY
EXPLORED

The conversation in the group should be like the conversation at a dinner party where you, as the host, are encouraging your guests to express themselves. What is their presenting issue? What is their perspective on life? Participants must feel that their views are taken seriously and not dismissed.

EXPLAINING

Having begun to work out where the participants are, we seek to move them on from this position. So we ask ourselves 'How do I apply the Christian message to this person's situation?'

So having listened to the participants and discerned their presenting issues, we then ask ourselves:

• Where is this person stuck?

• What is the Christian truth that they need to hear to enable them to grow in the 'knowledge of the truth that leads to godliness'? (Tit. 1:1)

Think of an unbelieving friend that you know well. Think about that person's presenting issues and then decide which of the truths in the framework of **2 ways to live** that person next needs to hear. Putting things very simply, if their struggle is with suffering, then they need to understand the consequences of human sin (box 2). We live in a cursed world (Gen. 3) awaiting its redemption (Rom. 8:18-25). If their struggle is with the existence of God, then they need to confront the risen Christ (box 5). If their struggle is with believing that God could care for them, then they need to understand the cross (box 4).

Throughout the course, as you come to pray at 6.30 p.m., think of where the participants are on the outline and pray for an opportunity to 'supply what is lacking' in their understanding (1 Thes. 3:10). We must always be asking ourselves, 'What is their next step in Christian understanding? Where is this person stuck?'

Sometimes a leader will sit down with a participant during the course and go through the **2 Ways to Live** outline with them on a piece of paper. This can be a great help to participants in diagnosing exactly where they are at in their understanding.

The framework can also be used to lead a participant to Christ using the A, B, C, D model:

A - Accept I've sinned (box 2)
B - Believe Christ died for me (box 4)
C - Count the cost of coming under Jesus' authority (box 6), using Mark 8:34
D - Do it! Come to Christ (box 6), using Revelation 3:20

It is important to emphasise, however, that this outline is no substitute for the work of the Holy Spirit. It is only as the Holy Spirit opens minds and hearts that people become receptive to the truth of Scripture. That is why it is essential that we are constantly in prayer for the participants. Pray that God would make their minds open to his truth. Pray that we, as leaders, will depend utterly on God's Holy Spirit for the words to speak and an appropriate Bible verse to teach.

ENCOURAGING

We encourage the participants to act upon God's truth, sharing our own struggles to trust and obey the Lord Jesus Christ in the process.

Some of the participants may face a real struggle as they embrace the truth of Christianity. Acting on these truths is no easy task because it will entail the 'obedience that comes through faith' (Rom. 1:5). These people need to be reassured and encouraged to hold on to their faith and to keep their confidence, for the Lord will reward it (Heb. 10:35).

At the heart of our encouragement is our own example and our own struggle to trust and obey. Those in our groups must feel that we are in the trenches with them. We are all struggling together in our pursuit to know Christ better. To be open with our own struggles, we need to understand that we are what Dietrich Bonhoeffer calls 'a community of truth'. As he says, 'The cross releases us to be unafraid of the truth about ourselves.' Grace tells us we're loved anyway, so let's not be afraid of talking through our own battles. It is a great help to the participants as we do so.

In this sense, our example is one of brokenness before God. Paul says that as believers we have been given the 'light of the knowledge of the glory of God in the face of Christ' (2 Cor. 4:6). He goes on, 'But we have this treasure in jars of clay to show that this all-surpassing power is from God and not from us.' (2 Cor. 4:7) We are very weak vessels, **but it is only through a cracked and broken pot that God's light will shine**. And it is in our weakness and dependency on God's strength that he is glorified and others will be drawn to him.

PERSONAL STUDY

Prior to the next training session you should:

• Learn the *2 Ways to Live* outline, so that all leaders have it as a framework of reference for teaching the gospel and for identifying participants' current issues.

CHRISTIANITY
EXPLORED

• Answer the eight introductory questions to Mark (see below). At the second training session, each group will have the opportunity to discuss and put together their best answers to these questions. (It is crucial that this work is done in advance, as there will only be 25 minutes available at the session itself to talk through each other's answers.)

KEY THEMES IN MARK

QUESTIONS FOR LEADERS

1 Mark 1:1; 8:29 and 15:37-39 are crucial signposts in the way Mark has constructed his Gospel. What do they suggest the main points of the Gospel are? What should we expect to see in the rest of the Gospel as Mark unpacks these points?

2 What sort of things do we see Jesus doing in the first half of the Gospel? (E.g. Mk. 1:16-26; 2:1-12; 4:1-9, 35-39; 6:35-44.) What does this teach us about what Jesus is like?

3 Apart from his miracles, what other evidence is there that Jesus
  really is the Christ, the Son of God?
  (E.g. Mk. 1:2-11; 9:2-7; 15:38; 16:4-7).

4 In the first part of the Gospel, how much do the disciples
  understand of who Jesus is? Why is this the case? (See Mk. 4:40-41;
  6:35-37, 52; 8:17-21.) What does Jesus do about their lack of
  understanding? (E.g. Mk. 4:33-34; 8:17-30).

5 How much do most of the Jews (including their leaders)
  understand of who Jesus is? (E.g. Mk. 2:6-7; 3:6; 8:11-12; 12:13-17;
  14:55-65.) To what extent does this matter? (Mk. 12:1-12).

6 What sort of things do we see Jesus teaching and doing in the second half of the Gospel? (E.g. Mk. 8:31-38; 9:30-37; 10:28-45.) What does this teach us about what Jesus is like? How can we reconcile the pictures we have of Jesus from the first and second halves of the Gospel?

7 How much more do the disciples understand in the second half of the Gospel? (E.g. Mk. 8:31-32; 9:31-32; 10:32-34.) Why does this lack of proper understanding matter? (Mk. 14:66-72).

8 Attempt a brief summary of Mark's purpose in writing this Gospel.

TEACHING
MARK'S GOSPEL

TALK 1:

WARNINGS FROM THE SOWER (MK. 4)

Understanding Mark chapter 4 is essential because it helps Christian workers get their expectations right. The context is one of opposition and misunderstanding and it follows chapter 3 where:

- the authorities want Jesus dead (Mk. 3:6);
- the people want miracles (Mk. 3:9-10);
- the disciples seem a hopeless lot, personified by Judas (Mk. 3:19);
- Jesus' family think he is mad (Mk. 3:21) and, most striking of all,
- the teachers of the law think he is possessed by the devil (Mk. 3:22).

The situation seems hopeless, and what is Jesus' response? To teach the word: 'With many similar parables Jesus spoke the word to them, as much as they could understand' (Mk. 4:33).

So his reaction to all these pressures is to teach. This small, supposedly insignificant seed - the word - will do its work. There are three reactions which Jesus (who is the farmer in the passage) met in his ministry and they will also be what we, his followers, are to expect when we call men and women to repent and believe because the kingdom has come (Mk. 1:15).

1 DISAPPOINTMENT

There will be negative as well as positive reactions to the word:

- the path (Mk. 4:15)
- the rocky places (Mk. 4:16)
- the thorns (Mk. 4:18).

This means that our work will contain heartbreak and disappointment. Sometimes those that come will be just like King Herod in Mark 6:20: 'Herod feared John and protected him, knowing him to be a righteous and holy man. When Herod heard John, he was greatly puzzled; yet he liked to listen to him.' Herod was gripped and yet, because of the influence of Herodias, his own drunkenness and peer pressure, he turned away. Unless we appreciate that there will be weeks when people in our groups do not turn up, then the disappointments could crush us.

2 DELAY

The metaphor from agriculture makes it obvious that it takes time for the seed to grow. You cannot plant and harvest on the same day. The farmer has to be patient because there is delay: 'Night and day, whether he sleeps or gets up, the seed sprouts and grows, though he does not know how' (Mk. 4:27). The problem is that the farmer cannot see this happening. He just has to trust that it is happening, so the emphasis is on patient waiting, making sure we don't get bored and give up. We simply have to play our part in planting the seed (the word) properly and trust God to play his part in bringing the seed to life.

The key thing to appreciate is that we live in an **instant** culture - **instant** news, **instant** food, **instant** information - and the participants may expect **instant** relationships with God. Like the Guinness advert, we have to keep reminding ourselves that 'good things come to those who wait'. Of course, the church is also immersed in this culture, and there is a temptation to try to provide instant results, but that is not faithful to the metaphor of the field in this parable. The law of the field is that you have to plough, plant, water, wait and then harvest. So if participants say, 'Well, I went along for one night, and it didn't work', actually they haven't tried it; just as any human relationship needs time, so the word needs time. This may mean that, as a leader, you have to stay in touch with the participants for weeks, months or even years after the course ends. Delay is necessary in the farmer's work and in **our** work.

'Others, like seed sown on good soil, hear the word, accept it, and produce a crop - thirty, sixty or even a hundred times what was sown' (Mk. 4:20).

The seed - God's word - delivers a dramatic harvest. Note the contrast between the tiny source and the immense conclusion: 'It is like a mustard seed, which is the smallest seed you plant in the ground. Yet when planted, it grows and becomes the largest of all garden plants, with such big branches that the birds of the air can perch in its shade' (Mk. 4:31-32).

This tiny seed becomes a mighty tree. It can all seem so pointlessly small at the start, as we sit around and teach a book written two thousand years ago about a crucified Galilean carpenter. Yet, the seed grows. The word does its work and the smallest seed becomes the biggest tree.

In his biography, *The Making of a Leader*, John Stott describes how a youth worker directed him to Revelation 3:20 when he was a schoolboy: 'So that night at my bedside, I made the experiment of faith and opened the door to Christ. I saw no flash of lightning, heard no peels of thunder, felt no electric shock pass through my body. In fact, I had no emotional experience at all. I just crept into bed and went to sleep.' If we had been there to witness that moment of a sixteen-year-old boy kneeling by his bed, we would not have concluded that it was one of the most significant moments in the history of the church in the twentieth century. But the word does its work and the seed grows. This is a striking example that there is nothing more powerful than the word.

We must keep planting the word in people's lives, for 'it will not return empty' (Is. 55:11). It is essential to realise that it is the word (the seed, v. 31) which produces God's reign (the kingdom, v. 30) in men and women's lives. So if the seed is not planted the kingdom cannot grow. The power is in the seed, the word of God, and we just have to teach it faithfully.

DISCUSSION OF PERSONAL STUDY

With these three expectations in place - **disappointments, delay** and **dramatic results** - please turn to the eight questions designed to give an overview of Mark's Gospel that you were asked to prepare for this session. We will get together in groups now and pool the best answers.

CHRISTIANITY
EXPLORED

TALK 2:

KEY THEMES IN MARK

Do you remember the scene in Titanic when the ship's designer realises that it is a mathematical certainty that the Titanic will sink within an hour? None of the passengers know this. They are blind to the reality of their fate.

Question 1 deals with this theme of blindness. The crucial signposts in Mark's Gospel are so obvious:

• Jesus is the Son of God (Mk. 1:1);
• He is recognised as the Christ (Mk. 8:29);
• He is the Christ, but his mission is to suffer and die, thereby opening up the way back to God (Mk. 15:37-39).

Question 2 reaffirms Jesus' identity further. We see that in the first half of the Gospel he acts as a man with supreme authority. We see his authority:

• to call people (Mk. 1:16-20);
• to teach (Mk. 1:21-22);
• over evil spirits (Mk. 1:25-26);
• to heal (Mk. 1:29-34);
• to forgive sins (Mk. 2:1-12);
• over nature (Mk. 4:35-39);
• over death (Mk. 5:35-42).

Question 3 further reveals a deluge of evidence about Jesus' identity apart from his miracles:

• there is the testimony of John the Baptist who, though surrounded by crowds, insists that he is not worthy to do up Jesus' shoes (Mk. 1:7);

• there is the witness of the Old Testament in which the prophets Malachi and Isaiah tell us that the Lord is coming to rescue (Is. 40:1-3) and judge (Mal. 3:1-5) his people. Both of those prophets are quoted in Mark 1:2-3;

• there is the witness of the Holy Spirit. As John insists, 'I baptise you with water but he will baptise you with the Holy Spirit' (Mk. 1:8);

• later there is the witness of Elijah and Moses at the transfiguration, accompanied by the voice from heaven which proclaims, 'This is my Son, whom I love. Listen to him!' (Mk. 9:7);

- the temple curtain is ripped from top to bottom (Mk. 15:38), revealing that the way into the presence of God, into the Holy of Holies, has been opened up;

- lastly, we have the witness of the young man dressed in a white robe in Mark 16:5, who tells us that Jesus has risen.

The evidence is overwhelming, and yet the disciples cannot see it (**Question 4**). This is why Jesus cries out in desperation in Mark 8:17-18: 'Do you still not see or understand? Are your hearts hardened? Do you have eyes that fail to see, and ears that fail to hear?' He had shown by the feeding of the 5,000 and 4,000 in the wilderness that he was the promised shepherd who would rescue his people, just as God had rescued the Israelites in the desert by feeding them with manna. And yet, the disciples cannot see the meaning of all his miracles. They cannot understand who he is, despite all the evidence. They are so blind.

It will take a miracle to get the disciples to see. This is why Jesus' frustration in Mark 8:17-18 is followed by the two-part healing of the blind man at Bethsaida. Jesus spits on the man's eyes, puts his hands on him and asks, 'Do you see anything?' (Mk. 8:23) Mark continues, 'He looked up and said, "I see people; they look like trees walking around." Once more Jesus put his hands on the man's eyes. Then his eyes were opened, his sight was restored, and he saw everything clearly.' (Mk. 8:24-25)

This two-part healing of the blind man is then played out in Peter's life. Peter is at the huge religious centre of Caesarea Philippi, named after Caesar in order to show that he was the ultimate god. In this centre of pluralism, Jesus asks, 'Who do you say I am?' and Peter answers, 'You are the Christ.' (Mk. 8:29) Peter's blind eyes have been *partially* opened. He can see Jesus is the Christ, the anointed king, but like the blind man in verse 24 his vision is impaired, for he cannot grasp the fact that Jesus must suffer and be killed (v. 31). That is not the Messiah that he wants, so in verse 32 he rebukes Jesus.

Thus we come to **Question 6** and Jesus' teaching in the second half of the Gospel.

The disciples have to see that they follow a suffering Messiah who has come to serve and die. It is not just the Jews (**Question 5**) who are blind, it is also the disciples. Throughout this book we see Jesus doing two things in order to get the disciples to see who he is:

- He speaks the word as much as they can understand (Mk. 4:33). Indeed, in Mark 1:38 he makes teaching and preaching his priority.

- He opens blind eyes. As we lead this course we have to have confidence in Jesus to do his work. That we can trust him is shown in the wonderful climax to the book, for there we see the Gentile centurion who headed the execution squad recognising that Jesus is the son of God (Mk. 15:39). That is a miracle. How can this centurion see that a naked, powerless, bleeding, dead, crucified Jew is the son of God? He can see it because God has opened his blind eyes. It is an amazing picture of grace; if God can reach out to the man who has just murdered his own son, then there is nobody beyond his grace.

Now if the disciples cannot see that Jesus is the Christ, that he had to suffer and die and that we in turn must take up our cross and follow him, then what happens? Consider Mark 14:66-72 (**Question 7**). Here Peter denies his faith in front of one of the most powerless people of the day - a servant girl. In verse 71 he calls down curses on himself and swears, 'I don't know this man you're talking about.' Peter is still partially blind, and, as the parable of the sower warned, he therefore denies Christ 'when trouble or persecution comes' (Mk. 4:17). Unless the participants are clear about who Jesus is, why he came and what it means to follow him, they, like Peter, will capitulate under the pressures which will inevitably come. They must be clearly rooted in these truths. This is why the ending of Mark's Gospel is so effective: 'Trembling and bewildered the women went out and fled from the tomb. They said nothing to anyone, because they were afraid.' (Mk. 16:8). The women flee because they have not understood; they are not clearly rooted in the crucial truths of Mark's Gospel. As we look at this passage with the participants we ask them clearly if they have understood it and if their roots are in place.

When Klebold and Harris, the two murderers from the Trench Coat Mafia, attacked Columbine High School in Colorado in 1998, an 18-year-old girl, Casey Bernall, was martyred. Eye witnesses report that Harris said to her, as he put a gun to her head, 'Who is your God? I must be your God because I am in total control.' Casey replied, 'You are not my God', and he killed her. Apparently Casey Bernall wanted to be a missionary. For that young girl to be martyred, to die rather than deny Christ, she had to understand all the teaching in Mark 8:27-38. Her blind eyes had been opened and she knew the answer to the three fundamental questions of this course:

- Who is Jesus? *Answer: the Christ (Mk. 8:29);*

- Why did he come? *Answer: to suffer and die (Mk. 8:31);*

- What does it mean to follow him? *Answer: deny yourself, take up your cross and lose your life (Mk. 8:34,35).*

Casey Bernall died because she knew that glory and triumph are not for this life but the life to come. Jesus tells us quite clearly that in this life we must be prepared to suffer and die for the gospel (**Question 6**). In Mark 8:38 he states clearly: 'If anyone is ashamed of me and my words in this adulterous and sinful generation, the Son of Man will be ashamed of him when he comes in his Father's glory with the holy angels.' The 'Son of Man' is a figure from Daniel 7:9-14 and we learn in Daniel that he reigns from the final judgement onwards. So what does Jesus do in this life? Answer: he suffers and dies. And what does he do in the next life? Answer: he reigns in glory.

If we are to produce authentic followers of Jesus, then they must see that, just as Jesus gave up his life in this world to reign over God's creation in the next, so we give up our lives in this world to enjoy God's creation in the next. That's what it means to follow him in this life, which is why Peter writes to those small struggling churches in Asia Minor, 'In this [your heavenly inheritance] you greatly rejoice, though now for a little while you may have had to suffer grief in all kinds of trials.' (1 Pet 1:6) **We have to be prepared to suffer and die for the gospel in this life**. That is the essence of Jesus' teaching from Mark 8:30 - 10:52 (**Question 6**). So he says to James and John, lobbying to sit on his left and right in glory, that they must drink the cup of suffering in this life (Mk. 10:39); and he calls us to a ruthless battle against sin (Mk. 9:42-48).

There are, of course, wonderful joys in becoming a Christian. We are given the gift of the Holy Spirit (Mk. 1:8); we receive forgiveness of sins (Mk. 2:10) and we can know that we have eternal life (Mk. 10:29-30). Nonetheless, it can be very hard, for there is much opposition. Our job is to communicate the 'bumped knee syndrome'. If a young child falls over and bumps his knee, all he can think of is the pain. We pick him up, cuddle him and know that he will be OK in half an hour. But he just feels the pain. We tell him he'll be fine but he continues to wail. If only he could see that he will be fine in half an hour. Paul sums it up in 2 Corinthians 4:17, when he calls all the terrible suffering of his life 'light and momentary troubles'.

As people come to *Christianity Explored*, particularly in the first week, we are concerned with their perceived needs. That is why we ask: 'If God was here and you could ask him any question and you knew that he would answer it, what would it be?' Ultimately, however, we have to show that the Son of Man holds the future. Though they may have to suffer grief in all kinds of trials for a little while now, if they retain the 'bumped knee' perspective for their brief lifetime they will cope and go on serving, whatever the pain. If they really come to understand this, then we will produce committed Christians who will change the nation.

You might think people will never accept this radical call to discipleship. Surely if we cut the price, more will buy? Do we really have to teach the call to cut off that which causes you to sin in Mark 9, or heed Jesus' words to the rich young man in Mark 10:21: 'Go, sell everything you have and give to the poor, and you will have treasure in heaven. Then come, follow me'? Surely if we are this radical, people will never accept it? It is precisely in response to these issues that Mark ends this section with the story of blind Bartimaeus (Mk. 10:46-52). Like blind Bartimaeus, and the disciples, **we need Jesus to open our eyes (Question 7), so we can see a Messiah who has come to die and expects his disciples to be prepared to do likewise**.

It takes a miracle for us:

1 to see Jesus;
2 to understand what he came to do and
3 take on board what it means to follow him.

Because of this we have to rely utterly on the work of the Holy Spirit throughout the course. We must pray that the Holy Spirit will convict the participants of sin, convince them of truth and convert them. And, as we pray, we teach, teach, teach. At the heart of the teaching is, of course, the heart of the gospel - that Jesus Christ is Lord. We must lay the foundation of Christ's lordship in their lives, 'for we do not preach ourselves, but Jesus Christ as Lord, and ourselves as your servants for Jesus' sake' (2 Cor. 4:5).

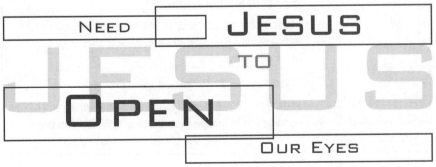

WE NEED JESUS TO OPEN OUR EYES

THE STRUCTURE
OF MARK'S GOSPEL

The objective of *Christianity Explored* is that at the end of Week 6 each participant has really grasped who Jesus is, why he came, and what it means to follow him. To that end, Mark is divided into four sections, which we work through in Weeks 1-6. (See table on pages 66 and 67.)

PART 1

JESUS SHOWS HE IS THE MESSIAH (MK. 1:1 - 8:29)

SECTION 1 (WEEK 1)

Mark 1:1 - 3:6 *Jesus comes on the scene and begins to reveal who he is but he is rejected by the Jewish authorities.*

SECTION 2 (WEEKS 2 AND 3)

Mark 3:7 - 8:29 *Jesus gathers a people to whom he reveals who he is and what he has come to do.*

PART 2

JESUS' MISSION AND THE NATURE OF DISCIPLESHIP (MK. 8:30 - 16:8)

SECTION 1 (WEEK 4)

Mark 8:30 - 10:52 *Jesus then teaches his disciples that in this world he must suffer and die and that they, too, must suffer with him.*

SECTION 2 (WEEKS 5 AND 6)

Mark 11:1 - 16:8 *Jesus goes to Jerusalem to die at the hands of the Jewish authorities and so fulfil God's purposes.*

CHRISTIANITY
EXPLORED

In their **Study Guide** the participants are given questions to help them discover the thrust of Mark's teaching in each section for themselves. They can jot down any questions which arise in their study and raise them at the beginning of the next session. The Study Guide also contains an overview to understanding Mark's Gospel as a whole and questions on the key themes of Mark for those who wish to continue with a more in-depth study.

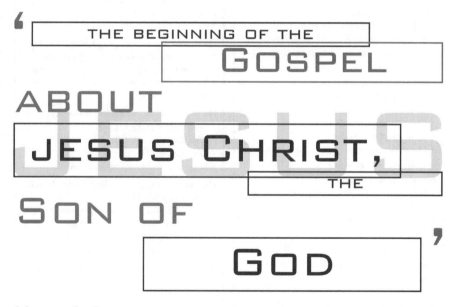

' THE BEGINNING OF THE GOSPEL ABOUT JESUS CHRIST, THE SON OF GOD '

MARK 1:1

SUMMARY OF MARK'S GOSPEL

Mark 1:1-3:6

Jesus comes on the scene and begins to reveal who he is, but he is rejected by the Jewish authorities

Jesus is the Christ, the Son of God
- This is how Mark introduces his gospel (1:1)
- This is attested by the Old Testament which John the Baptist too is fulfilling (1:2-8) and God (1:9-11)

Jesus shows his authority
- Over people (e.g. 1:16-20)
- Over evil spirits (e.g. 1:21-26)
- Over illness (e.g. 1:40-45)
- To forgive sin (2:1-12)
- Over the Jew's religion, e.g. the Sabbath (2:27-28)

Jesus' ministry
- Is to teach (1:14-15) and this is his priority (1:35-39)
- Is to everyone, even outcasts from the establishment (2:17)
- Is inaugurating something new (2:21-22)

The Jews growing hostility
- Because they do not like what he is doing (e.g. 2:15-17)
- Culminating in their plot to kill Jesus (3:6)

Mark 3:7-8:29

Jesus gathers a people to whom he reveals who he is and what he has come to do

Jesus calls the Twelve to be God's true people (3:13-19, 31-35)
- Because the Jews are rejecting him

Jesus then focuses on these disciples
- He teaches them clearly, but the crowds only in parables (4:1-34)
- The disciples see his miracles but the Jews don't (e.g. 6:47-51)

He continues to reveal his authority
- Over nature (4:35-41)
- Over evil spirits (5:1-21)
- Over death (5:35-43)
- In creating from nothing (6:35-44)

He has come to rescue God's people in a 'second Exodus' (6:32-44)
- Jesus is the good shepherd promised for the time when God will rescue Israel
- The feeding of the crowd is like the feeding of the Israelites in the Exodus

The disciples struggle to grasp who Jesus is
- This is due to lack of faith that understands (e.g. 4:40-41)
- Jesus works to get his disciples to understand who he is (e.g. 8:17-21)
- Eventually they see that Jesus is the Christ, but this takes a miracle (8:22-29)
- Christ is the king promised in the Old Testament who will rescue God's people

MARK'S

GOSPEL TELLS US

CHRISTIANITY EXPLORED

Mark 8:30-10:52

Jesus then teaches his disciples that in this world he must suffer and die and that they too must suffer with him

Jesus is the Son of Man and the Son of God
- Son of Man (e.g. 8:31) is a reference to Daniel 7:9-14 where the Son of Man is the king who will rule over everyone forever, after the final judgement
- 'Son' is what God calls Jesus (9:2-7), indicating his divinity

But in this world he must suffer and die (e.g. 8:31, 9:31, 10:33-34)
- As Son of Man he will rule in the next world, but in this world he must suffer and only enter his reign through his resurrection
- But the disciples can't grasp that Jesus must die in this world (e.g. 9:31-32)

Being a disciple means being prepared to suffer and die with Jesus (e.g. 8:34, 10:42-45)
- Those who are not prepared to give up their lives in this world will not enjoy life in the next (e.g. 8:35-38)
- But the disciples can't grasp that they are called to be different, so they seek honour for themselves (e.g. 9:33-35, 10:35-41)

Mark 11:1-16:8

Jesus goes to Jerusalem to die at the hands of the Jewish authorities and so fulfil God's purposes

Jesus goes to Jerusalem to condemn the Jews for their rejection of him
- The Jews are rebelling against God and their killing of Jesus will be the climax of this rebellion (e.g. 12:1-8)
- But God will judge the Jews and choose a different people (e.g. 12:9-11)

Jesus then goes to his death
- It is a very costly thing (e.g. 14:32-36, 15:34)
- But it is not a mistake nor an accident, he is in total control (e.g. 14:12-30)
- His death accomplishes God's rescue of his people (e.g. 14:24, 15:38)
- In his death he is finally seen for who he is by the Gentile centurion (15:39)

But his disciples are still confused and weak
- They all desert him (e.g. 14:50, 64-72)
- Even at the end they don't understand (16:8)
- But the two-part miracle of 8:22-26 indicates that they will come to understand

He tells his disciples what life will be like after his death and before his return
- It will be a difficult time (e.g. 13:5-13)
- Jesus' disciples must stand firm (e.g. 13:13, 22-23)

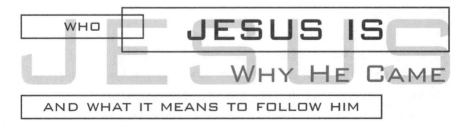

WHO **JESUS IS**
WHY HE CAME

AND WHAT IT MEANS TO FOLLOW HIM

MEETING CHRIST IN MARK

Mark opens with the words: 'The beginning of the gospel about Jesus Christ, the Son of God.' It is a book about the great news of Jesus, and in particular about who he is - the divine Christ who has come to rescue God's people and judge his enemies, as the Old Testament predicted.

This profound and fabulous truth lies at the heart of all four gospels, but Mark is the shortest and most straightforward. The gospels are the pinnacle of Scripture and are actually harder to understand than we often think. However, they are the best place to get a really clear grasp of who Jesus is and it makes sense to start with the simplest of them.

Two key passages in the book help us grasp how Mark has constructed his gospel - Mark 8:27-29 and Mark 15:37-39. Effectively, the Gospel is split in two sections and the message of the first part culminates in Mark 8:27-29:

> Jesus and his disciples went on to the villages around Caesarea Philippi. On the way he asked them, 'Who do people say I am?' They replied, 'Some say John the Baptist; others say Elijah; and still others, one of the prophets.' 'But what about you?' he asked. 'Who do you say I am?' Peter answered, 'You are the Christ.'

The focus of the first half of Mark's Gospel is that Jesus is the Christ or Messiah.

But what does this mean, and how will he accomplish the predicted rescue and judgement? These ideas are introduced in the first part of the book but both are taken radically further in the second half of the gospel. The climax comes in Mark 15:37-39:

> With a loud cry, Jesus breathed his last. The curtain of the temple was torn in two from top to bottom. And when the centurion, who stood there in front of Jesus, heard his cry and saw how he died, he said, 'Surely this man was the Son of God!'

The focus of the second half of the Gospel is that Jesus is the divine Son of God, but that on earth he suffers and dies, and by doing this he opens the way into God's presence.

CHRISTIANITY
E✝PLORED

As we study Mark, it is also important for us to see how people come to grasp who Jesus is. This key feature of Mark's Gospel is highlighted in Peter's failure to recognise Jesus as the Christ until halfway through the Gospel account. Furthermore, the fact that he is recognised as the Son of God for the first time only as he breathes his last - and that by a Gentile - indicates that **recognising Jesus is not as straightforward as we might think.**

Understanding how people come to grasp who Jesus really is particularly interests us as we help the participants to see who Jesus is. We will discover that this involves not only hearing what he says and seeing what he does: it requires a miracle.

The summary of Mark's Gospel (pages 66 and 67) shows the division of the book into two main parts:

Part 1 - Jesus shows he is the Messiah;

Part 2 - Jesus' mission and the nature of discipleship.

This is split down further into four aspects of Jesus' ministry which we will consider in more detail here.

JESUS SHOWS HE IS THE MESSIAH: SECTION 1

MARK 1:1 - 3:6

The first 13 verses of this section are a prologue before Jesus begins his ministry. Mark makes three points here:

- In verses 2-3, he reminds us of the Old Testament prophecy about the messenger who announces the coming of the Lord who will judge and rescue.

- In verses 4-8, we see that John the Baptist fulfils this prophecy.

- Finally, in verses 9-12, we see that Jesus is the person whose way John the Baptist is preparing and God himself confirms this.

Mark 1:13 - 3:6 details the beginning of Jesus' ministry in a highly-condensed summary, which draws attention to four aspects in particular:

(a) Jesus demonstrates who he is through his remarkable authority:

- He calls people and they follow him immediately, abandoning what they were doing (e.g. Mk. 1:16-20);

- He commands evil spirits and they obey, against their wishes (e.g. Mk. 1:21-26);

- He heals major illnesses, with people immediately and demonstrably restored to total health (e.g. Mk. 1:40-44);

- He even has the authority to forgive sin (Mk. 2:1-12).

(b) Despite this amazing authority, Jesus' primary purpose is not to solve the many and varied problems of this world, but to teach that God's plans are now being fulfilled so everyone should repent and believe. This striking truth can be seen both in the summary of his ministry in Mark 1:14-15, and in the remarkable incident detailed in Mark 1:35-39 when Jesus shows the priority of preaching over healing.

(c) Jesus goes to **all** the people of Israel, even to those commonly thought of as outcasts, such as lepers (Mk. 1:40) and sinners (Mk. 2:15). He goes as far as to state that these outcasts are most need of what he has to offer (Mk. 2:17).

(d) Jesus ignores many of the religious observances the Jews cherish, for example, fasting (Mk. 2:18-19) and Sabbath observance (Mk. 2:23-24). He proclaims not only authority over their rites, but the ability to supersede them.

In general, the people are amazed at what he is doing (e.g. Mk. 2:12) and come in droves to hear him. However, the religious authorities object to some of his claims (e.g. Mk. 2:6-7) and dislike the fact that he is not obeying the detailed religious code to which they have given their lives (e.g. Mk. 2:24). In the end, they decide to try to kill him (Mk. 3:6). This is a striking development so early on in the Gospel. It shapes much of what follows, as Jesus withdraws from the religious leaders (Mk. 3:7) and has minimal contact with them until he has called and trained a new people for himself. Then, ready to meet his death, he confronts them in Jerusalem, as shown in chapters 11 - 16.

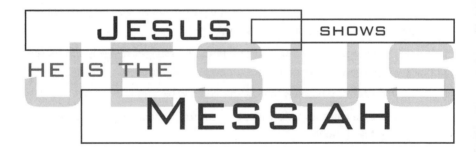

JESUS SHOWS HE IS THE MESSIAH

MARK 3:7 - 8:29

These verses form the foundation on which the rest of the Gospel is built. Here Jesus displays his greatest miracles, reveals what he has come to accomplish and brings his disciples to understand who he is. The four things Mark particularly wants us to see are:

(a) Jesus is now focusing his energies on his disciples:

- The section begins with Jesus withdrawing from the Jewish authorities. On the few occasions that they appear after this they are not the focus of interest until chapter 11.

- In Mark 3:13-19, Jesus appoints twelve disciples, symbolising a new, true Israel which will replace the original Israel founded on twelve tribes.

- By Mark 3:31-35, Jesus states that his true family are not blood relations, but those who do God's will.

- From chapter 4 onwards Jesus teaches the crowds in parables which he explains only to his disciples (Mk. 4:33-34). His disciples have the secret of God's kingdom, but those who are not his disciples are only taught in parables so they **cannot** understand (Mk. 4: 10-12)

- Many of Jesus' miracles from this point onwards are seen primarily by the disciples and not the Jews generally - e.g. in Mark 4:35-39 only those in the boat with Jesus would have heard him stop the storm, and in Mark 5:1-13 Jesus is in Gentile territory so no Jews (other than his disciples) would have seen him cast the evil spirits out of Legion, the demon-possessed man.

It may seem a major retrograde step for Jesus to be focusing on a handful of disciples when he had previously had a great and successful ministry to many thousands of people, but these disciples are the beginning of Jesus' new people. This brings us to Mark's second point, which comes in chapter 4. In the parables about God's kingdom, Jesus teaches us that this is what it is like. It does involve much waste - there can be heart-breaking disappointment in the way some respond to the word. It does start very small. It does grow gradually, without any fanfare and in ways we don't understand. But in the end it will be a great kingdom.

(b) Jesus' remarkable authority is shown in even clearer terms:

- He has authority over nature (Mk. 4:35-39) which enables him to completely calm a 'furious squall' - a major feat since waves normally persist long after a wind dies down.

- He has total authority over evil spirits so powerful that even chains could not bind the man they possess (Mk. 5:2-13).

- He has authority to instantly and totally conquer death, the greatest of enemies (Mk. 5:35-43).

- He is able to feed crowds of many thousands with only a couple of small fish and a few loaves of bread, displaying creation out of nothing (Mk. 6:35-44; 8:1-9).

(c) Jesus reveals what he has come to do, namely to rescue God's people. We need to understand the Old Testament to grasp this as Mark's original readers would have done. Towards the end of the Old Testament Israel was conquered by her enemies and taken into exile. However, God promised through the prophets that this was not the end and that he would one day rescue her from this exile and bless her enormously. Israel returned from her exile in Babylon more than five hundred years before Jesus lived on earth, but the prophets' promises were never fulfilled. The Jews were therefore waiting for the 'real return' from exile and this expectation was one of the most dominant forces shaping their culture. Their expectation of the Messiah was linked to this, since God had said that the return from exile would be associated with the coming of the Messiah (e.g. Is. 9:1-7).

From the middle of chapter 6 to the middle of chapter 8, Jesus alludes to several of the Old Testament promises about what will happen when the exile really ends, and he shows that they are being fulfilled in him. Three of the most important of these are:

- In Ezekiel 34 God describes exiled Israel as sheep without a shepherd (e.g. Ezek. 34:5) and says that one day he will shepherd Israel himself through the Messiah (e.g. Ezek. 34:23). Jesus picks this idea up in Mark 6:34 and takes on the role of God's good shepherd.

- In passages like Isaiah 11:11-16 God says that when he rescues Israel from exile it will be a second exodus, i.e. a rescue like the one God performed when he rescued Israel from Egypt at the beginning of her history. In Mark 6:32-44, Jesus feeds the crowds in a manner reminiscent of the way that God fed Israel with manna in the desert. This may seem obscure to us but it is a key miracle - the only one recorded in all four gospels.

CHRISTIANITY
E✗PLORED

- The prophet Isaiah regularly describes God's people as blind and deaf because of their refusal to see and hear what God is doing (e.g. Is. 6:9-10). However, he also says that when God rescues his people he will open their blind eyes and deaf ears (e.g. Is. 29:18; 32:3; 35:5). This appears to be what Jesus is doing in the miracles (e.g. Mk. 7:32-35; 8:22-25). This idea is confirmed in Mark 7:32, where Mark uses a very rare Greek word that was also used in the Greek version of Isaiah 35:5.

(d) Mark wants us to see that the disciples struggle to understand who Jesus is, despite all the evidence, but they do eventually get there. Throughout this section, the question on everyone's lips is, 'Who is he?' The disciples (Mk. 4:41), the people, and even King Herod (Mk. 6:14-16), speculate about who Jesus is. In Mark 8:27-29 Jesus himself discusses his identity with the disciples.

But why is it so difficult for everyone to see who he is? The answer Jesus gives is 'lack of faith', and all the way through this section we see that faith is the right response to Jesus. The woman in Mark 5:25-34 is healed by faith; the synagogue ruler is told to have faith, in Mark 5:36; the disciples are rebuked for lack of faith in Mark 4:40. In fact, Jesus specifically rebukes his disciples for lack of understanding (e.g. Mk. 8:17-21) and the Bible never makes a distinction between faith and understanding. The disciples need faith to understand that Jesus is doing all the things that God said the Messiah would do, so he must be the Messiah.

How can the disciples' blind eyes be opened to see who Jesus is? Jesus challenges the disciples to think about what he is doing (e.g. Mk. 8:17-21), but it takes more than this. It takes a miracle. This is the point Jesus is making in the two miracles of opening the deaf man's ears and opening the blind man's eyes (Mk. 7:32-35 and Mk. 8:22-25). The fact that these are the only miracles Jesus shows any difficulty in carrying out indicates how hard it is to get people to see who he is. Note how Peter grasps who Jesus is immediately after the blind man's eyes are opened: in just the same way as the blind man, he sees only partially at first. In the next section Peter reveals the gaps in his understanding, but what he has grasped is that Jesus is God's promised Messiah who has come to rescue God's people and so fulfil all that God has promised in the Old Testament.

As we teach our participants we will also find that **getting them to grasp that Jesus is the Christ in whom they must have faith will require both hard work in teaching them on our part and a miracle that only God can do**.

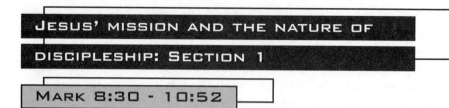
MARK 8:30 - 10:52

At the end of the previous section the disciples eventually grasp that Jesus is the Christ who will rescue God's people. But Jesus has much more to reveal about the sort of Christ he is, how he will perform this rescue and what it means to be his disciple. Immediately Peter recognises that he is the Christ, Jesus moves on to this, teaching his disciples three very radical truths:

(a) He is the Son of Man and the Son of God. Jesus begins to refer to himself regularly as 'Son of Man' and also takes his closest disciples up the mountain to see him being transfigured and called 'Son' by God himself. Both these titles go further than 'Christ' or 'Messiah' in two important ways.

- The 'Son of Man' is given everlasting rule over the whole world in Daniel 7:9-14. While there are hints earlier in the Old Testament that the Messiah will rule over other nations as well as Israel, Daniel is absolutely explicit about how infinitely far-reaching the reign of God's king will be. However, there is one crucial thing to note about the rule of the Son of Man in Daniel 7: it begins at the final judgement. Jesus, the Son of Man, comes to reign from the judgement onwards; if I follow him in this life I will suffer as he suffers, but I will enjoy his rule for the judgement.

- Jesus is divine, as shown in Mark 9, where God calls Jesus 'Son' and Jesus is transfigured to look like God himself, as described in Daniel 7:9. The Old Testament does say that the Messiah will be divine, but not often. The Jews of Jesus' day appear to have ignored this fact, and when Jesus appears and is acknowledged as divine by God, this would have shocked the staunchly monotheistic Jews.

(b) He must suffer and die. The Old Testament predicted that the Messiah would die in order to accomplish God's rescue plan and he would only be recognised as king after his resurrection (Is. 53:10-12). Jesus teaches his disciples this truth three times (Mk. 8:31; 9:31; 10:33-34) and refers to it on other occasions. In Mark 10:45 he explains why he has to die: he has come to serve, and in particular to serve by giving his life as a ransom for other people.

CHRISTIANITY
EXPLORED

However, Jesus' disciples totally fail to understand what he is saying (Mk. 8:32; 9:32) and this failure to understand matters enormously. When Peter has the temerity to rebuke Jesus for saying he will die, Jesus is scathing in his retort, calling Peter 'Satan' and accusing him of being concerned about man's agenda, not God's (Mk. 8:33). This ought to make us pause and repent, since we very often think like Peter does here and fail to see that in God's plan, glory and triumph are not for this life, but the life to come.

(c) The disciples, too, must humble themselves, serve others, and be prepared to suffer and die (Mk. 8:34-38). Just as Jesus is giving up his life in this world in order to reign over God's new creation, so his disciples must give up their lives in this world if they want to enjoy God's new creation. Jesus expands this idea further, teaching in Mark 9:42-50 that anything - even physical maiming - is better than failing to obtain this eternal new creation. Again, in Mark 10:17-31, Jesus emphasises that it is worth giving up all material possessions in order to gain eternal life.

However, Jesus is under no illusion that this is going to be easy. In fact, in his teaching on divorce, he shows how high God's moral standards are in other areas of life as well. So how can anyone be saved if standards this impossibly high are being set? That is exactly what the disciples ask when they first hear Jesus' teaching: 'Who then can be saved?' (Mk. 10:26). He answers that it is indeed impossible for anyone to be saved by living up to these standards, but it is possible for God to save people. It is possible because Jesus is going to die as a ransom for his people (Mk. 10:45) and because God can help people to follow Jesus even when they know what the potential cost might be.

It is important to see that we are walking a tightrope here. On the one hand, we must not give people the impression that anyone can live up to God's perfect standards and demands, even as a Christian. Most Christians will not be physically maimed or forced to give up all that they own. We are not teaching that we are saved because we can be good enough - albeit with God's help. On the other hand, however, we must help people see that being a Christian is not an easy option. It will demand our whole lives and we *may* be required to give up all our wealth or even to be maimed. We do not want to produce people who think they are Christians but are not, because they are not willing to lose their lives for Jesus and the gospel (Mk. 8:35). This is one of the most common problems today in many of our churches.

This sort of radical willingness to give up our lives in this world is, of course, directly contrary to the way the world thinks. Things were no different in Jesus' day so it is not surprising that the disciples find Jesus' teaching on discipleship very hard to accept. This comes through clearly in Mark 9:33-37 and Mark 10:35-45, where they seem unable to grasp the concept of self-sacrifice, or the fact that Jesus himself must give up his life on earth. However, despite this discouraging situation, the section ends with the miracle of Jesus healing a blind man - a reminder that God alone can help anyone see who Jesus is.

The two-part healing in Mark 8:22-25 is being played out in the disciples' lives. They have understood that Jesus is the Messiah but not yet that he is a Messiah who will die and who expects his disciples to be prepared to do likewise. As it took a miracle to achieve the first level of understanding, so it will take a miracle for the second. Fortunately, to God all things are possible.

JESUS' MISSION AND THE NATURE OF DISCIPLESHIP: SECTION 2

MARK 11:1 - 16:8

In the final section of the Gospel we see Jesus go to Jerusalem to pass judgement on the Jews and to accomplish the rescue of God's true people. Though there is still some teaching of his disciples in private, this teaching has almost finished and the balance has shifted. Jesus returns to the public arena and spends most of his time teaching everyone.

The parable in Mark 12:1-11 is key to understanding this section. Together with the similar enacted parable of the cursed fig-tree, it explains much of what is happening in the rest of the section, particularly with regard to Jesus' relationship with the Jews. The vineyard in the parable represents Israel, an illustration made explicit in the Old Testament (e.g. Is. 5:1-7). Jesus is the son, God is the owner and the servants who are sent initially to collect fruit are the Old Testament prophets. The tenants are the Jewish establishment, i.e. the leaders and their followers - all those who bay for Jesus' blood in Mark 15:11-15.

Thus, Jesus is coming to Israel to collect the fruit of obedience and trust that God has always demanded from his people but they have so seldom given him. However, instead of honouring him, the Jews reject and kill him. We see this rejection as Jesus teaches in the temple, when they question his authority and try to trap him, despite his history of tremendous miracles. In line with the parable, he is arrested, subjected to a farce of a trial, and crucified to satisfy the crowds' demands, despite his innocence. As a result, God will take the privilege of being God's people away from those unbelieving Jews and give it to others - to Jesus' disciples, the new Israel that he has been calling and teaching (Mk. 12:9-11). We see this judgement on Israel symbolised when the darkness falls on the land as Jesus hangs dying on the cross (Mk. 15:33).

However, Jesus' death is more than an occasion for God to judge the Jews and give his kingdom to others; it is the means by which God accomplishes the rescue of his people that he has planned since the beginning of time and that Jesus came to bring about.

It is important to recognise that Jesus is not simply a helpless victim of circumstances, as the son in the parable might appear. He is in total control of his situation at all times and he goes to his death deliberately and purposefully. Note his detailed and exact prior knowledge of events: the colt he will ride into Jerusalem (Mk. 11:2); the imminence of his death (Mk. 14:8); the last Passover meal with his disciples (Mk. 14:13-16); Judas' betrayal (Mk. 14:18); the disciples' desertion (Mk. 14:27) and Peter's denial (Mk. 14:29-30).

More than this, everything Jesus is experiencing is predicted in the Old Testament, hundreds of years before it occurred. So he goes into Jerusalem, as the king predicted by the prophet Zechariah five hundred years previously (Zech. 9:9). He is rejected by the Jewish authorities, only to become the head of the new Israel, as foretold in Psalm 118. His disciples desert him as Zechariah predicted, and his death takes place as detailed in the Psalms, written centuries before Jesus was born.

So what is the significance of this death that Jesus deliberately faced and which is important enough for God to describe in advance in virtually all of its aspects? As we looked at the feeding of the 5,000 we saw that Jesus was coming to fulfil the Old Testament prophecy of a second exodus. The first exodus began with the original Passover when God judged Egypt but spared Israel because of the sacrifice of the Passover lamb. This event continued to be celebrated every year, and Jesus goes to his death at the time of the celebration, which symbolises his death as the inauguration of the second exodus (Mk. 14:12-25). This sacrifice also establishes the new covenant that the Old Testament had promised would be associated with this second exodus (Mk. 14:24, cf. (i.e. compare) Jer. 31:31-34). As a result, the people and God can now dwell together; the curtain in the temple that symbolised their separation is torn violently in two as Jesus dies (Mk. 15:38).

So Jesus goes to his death in control of his circumstances, in accordance with the Old Testament and to achieve the fulfilment of all that God has worked towards throughout the whole of history. However, this does not make the cross easy. It is a terrible thing for Jesus to be separated from God, and in the garden of Gethsemane we see him in anguish as he contemplates his death but nevertheless accepts God's will (Mk. 14:36).

The Gentile soldier's recognition of Jesus as the Son of God at the moment of his death (Mk. 15:39) is one of the most striking verses in the Gospel. How can anyone looking at that limp, broken body recognise that he is God's son? Jesus has been teaching since Mark 8:31 not only that he **must** suffer and die, but that it will take a miracle for anyone to grasp this. Here, as he dies, we see the miracle beginning to take place. **The Christ is totally different from the person the Jews had been expecting. Immeasurably greater, but humbling himself so much further** - none of them has fully recognised who he is. And yet, he is recognisable with God's help. God begins to help people recognise him at his moment of greatest suffering and greatest triumph.

However, all the way through this final section we see the disciples continued lack of understanding. They do not appreciate, for example, that Jesus is not concerned about earthly things, such as the Jews' magnificent temple (Mk. 13:1-2). They still do not grasp that Jesus is going to his death and doing this willingly, so they try to fight when he is arrested (Mk. 14:47). They have no perspective on how weak and fallible they are themselves, so when Jesus predicts that they will deny him, they refuse to accept it (Mk. 14:27-31). Because they are not prepared to give up their lives in this world, as Jesus had said was necessary, they run away and deny him (Mk. 14:50,71). Finally, and most strikingly, even when confronted with the empty tomb they fail to understand its meaning (Mk. 16:8).

What hope is there for these weak, slow disciples? The same hope there is for us - that God will open their eyes by the miracle that only he can perform (Mk. 8:22-25; 10:46-52). As Jesus said when he was asked who could be saved, 'With man this is impossible, but not with God; all things are possible with God' (Mk. 10:26-27).

FREQUENTLY ASKED
QUESTIONS FROM MARK

Michael Bennett ran the *Christianity Explained* course in Australia for 20 years and compiled this list of frequently asked questions from his experience of teaching Mark. While much of this material is covered in the leader's notes on individual Bible studies, this is a helpful reference for the questions which regularly come up during discussions.

1 WHAT ARE DEMONS, OR EVIL SPIRITS?
(MK. 1:23-27)

The Bible takes the reality of an unseen spiritual world seriously - in both its positive aspects and its evil or malignant side.

The devil, or Satan, is not just some impersonal evil force at work in the world. According to the Bible, Satan is a fallen angelic being, who is personal, powerful, in rebellion against God and hostile to God's people. Although Satan, and other fallen angels in alliance with him, are immensely powerful, the New Testament shows Jesus to be Lord over Satan and to have overcome him by the power of his death on the cross (Col. 2:15).

2 WHY DID JESUS TELL HEALED PEOPLE
NOT TO TELL ANYONE? (MK. 1:34; 7:36)

While Christ's healings were a necessary part of demonstrating the rule and kingdom of God, Jesus did not want to become a side-show, with people following him just to see signs and wonders. He rejected such people (Mk. 8:11-13; Jn. 4:48). If people would not respond to the preaching of the kingdom of God, which called for repentance and faith (Mk. 1:15), miracles alone would not convince them. **He had not come to perform miracles to satisfy people's curiosity, but to die for them.**

3 WHY DID JESUS CALL HIMSELF THE SON OF MAN? (MK. 2:10)

'Son of Man' is Jesus' favourite title for himself. There are two main reasons for this, both of which complement each other:

- Many Jews had the wrong idea of what the Messiah (i.e. Christ) would do. If Jesus had referred to himself as the Christ this would have led to even more confusion about who he was than there was already. It may even have led to him being executed even sooner as a blasphemous pretender, possibly before he was ready for it. While the title Son of Man was also a title for God's promised king, it was less value laden.

- The title 'Son of Man' comes from Daniel 7:13-14 where it refers to God's king who will rule over everyone forever, **starting from the final judgement**. This adds the vital idea that he will not necessarily be crowned king in this world, and is, of course, exactly what Jesus spends much of his time teaching. He is God's chosen king who will rule in glory, but in this world, far from ruling, he must suffer and die. Thus, 'Son of Man' is a fuller and more accurate description of who Jesus is, one which reflects exactly what Jesus is trying to teach his disciples.

4 WHAT DOES THE TEACHING ABOUT THE NEW CLOTH/OLD COAT AND NEW WINE/OLD SKINS MEAN? (MK. 2:21-22)

People were complaining that Jesus was not observing the religious rules and traditions of his day (Mk. 2:18). The Pharisees had literally thousands of laws and religious regulations and they taught that a person had to observe these rigorously in order to please God.

Jesus was saying that the faith that he had come to bring could not be 'fitted into' their legalistic religion. **He came to bring a living relationship with God, not rules; grace, love and peace, not religious formulae.**

Christianity is not a set of rules, but a personal relationship with the Living God.

CHRISTIANITY
E*X*PLORED

5 WHAT IS THE 'ETERNAL SIN'? (MK. 3:29)

The context here is the key. The religious leaders had observed Jesus' miracles and heard his teaching at first hand. However their assessment of Jesus was: 'He is possessed by Beelzebub' (Mk 3:22) - an old name for the devil.

They had hardened their hearts against the work of God's Spirit through the ministry of Jesus. This continuously unrepentant attitude is the 'blasphemy against the Holy Spirit' (Mk. 3:29). In simple terms it means to continuously reject Jesus' claim on a person's heart and life. For this there can be no forgiveness, for they have refused the only way of forgiveness that God has provided. Of course, it is only unforgivable for as long as a person goes on doing it. Many of the religious leaders did repent later, and so were forgiven (Acts 6:7).

This is a vital personal concept. If I reject Jesus, I can never be forgiven.

6 WHY DID JESUS TEACH IN PARABLES? (MK. 4:10-12)

Many people have trouble with this passage. On the surface, it appears as if Jesus taught in parables so that people would not understand, which would be very strange indeed. However, we need to see that there are two groups mentioned here: the disciples and 'those outside'. The disciples were spiritually intrigued by the parables and drew nearer to Jesus to hear the explanation. There is a spiritual principle here - 'to those who have, more will be given' (Mk. 4:25). However, to those who were not really interested, the parables just remained intriguing stories. They 'hear, but do not understand'.

We are all either like moths or bats: attracted to the light of Jesus' teaching or repelled by it. Jesus' words, including his parables, always act in this two-fold way. See also Mark 4:33-34.

7 DID JESUS HAVE BROTHERS AND SISTERS? (MK. 6:3)

This passage mentions four brothers by name and at least two sisters. It seems to have been his brother James who wrote the New Testament book by that name.

These were presumably the natural children of Joseph and Mary, conceived after the birth of Jesus. See also Mark 3:32. This helps to answer the question as to whether Mary remained a virgin after the birth of Jesus. In addition, Matthew 1:25 certainly implies that Joseph and Mary had a normal sexual relationship after Jesus' birth.

8 WHY DOES JESUS USE THE TERM 'DOGS'? (MK. 7:24-30)

The key to this difficult passage lies in the fact that the woman was not a Jewess - she was a Gentile from near the pagan city of Tyre (Mk. 7:24-26). Jesus' ministry at this stage was exclusively to the Jews, the chosen descendants of Abraham. He forbade his disciples, at this time, to preach to the Gentiles or Samaritans (Mt. 10:5).

Jesus says to her, 'Let us first feed the children. It isn't right to take the children's food and throw it to the dogs.' The term 'children' here refers to the Jews and 'dogs' was a common unflattering expression for any Gentile person. So Jesus is saying in fact, 'It isn't right to take what belongs to the Jews and give it to you Gentiles.'

In her reply in verse 28 the woman is, in effect, saying, 'Yes Lord - I acknowledge that as a Gentile woman I have no claim upon you, the Jewish Messiah. But at least give me a few moments of your time to deal with a problem I have!'

Jesus is impressed by her faith and her persistence and grants her request (Mk. 7:29).

The term 'dogs' was not used vindictively by Jesus. One writer says, 'The Lord's use of the conventional Jewish term dogs for Gentiles does not mean that he recognised this description as accurate. He desired to see whether the woman was ready to take such a lowly position in order to win healing.'

9 WHAT IS THE YEAST OF THE PHARISEES AND THE YEAST OF HEROD? (MK. 8:15)

Yeast means influence. Just as a tiny amount of yeast has a substantial effect on the whole batch of dough, so Jesus warns against the 'yeast' of the Pharisees and Herod. The Pharisees were the most influential religious party in Jesus' day, though they were few in number. They taught that rigorous law-keeping was the path to God. Jesus called them 'hypocrites', which means 'play-actors', because of their public displays of religion and self-righteousness.

With reference to the yeast of Herod, one writer says, 'The yeast of Herod is adultery, murder, hastiness in swearing, affectation in piety and hatred of Christ and his forerunner (John the Baptist).'

So Jesus is warning against outward religious show (the Pharisees) and crass worldliness (Herod). By contrast, he himself is concerned with the internal and spiritual, the permanent and eternal. If the disciples let the worldly thinking of the Pharisees and Herod influence them, they would never understand who Jesus is.

1 0 WHY SHOULD THE DISCIPLES UNDERSTAND WHO JESUS IS? (MK. 8:17-21)

Twice Jesus had fed large crowds of Jewish people in a desert place where no food was available. Surely, as Jews, they would have been reminded of the way God fed the children of Israel, under the leadership of Moses, by giving them the manna in the desert.

Surely, too, they would have remembered Moses' prophecy towards the end of his life: 'The Lord your God will raise up for you a prophet like me from among your own brothers' (Deut. 18:15). Could the disciples not yet understand that Jesus was the predicted Moses-like prophet and, beyond that, the prophesied Messiah? It is perhaps no accident that in the very next section Peter declares, 'You are the Messiah' (Mk. 8:29). The penny has dropped at last!

1 1 WHAT IS 'THE KINGDOM OF GOD COME WITH POWER'? (MK. 9:1)

This is probably a reference to the transfiguration which is recorded immediately after this (Mk. 9:2-7). Jesus has been revealing that he is the Son of Man who will rule in eternity but who will suffer and die in this world (Mk. 8:31-38). In order to confirm his disciples' new understanding that he is the Christ (Mk. 8:29), Jesus promises them a dress rehearsal of what he will be like when he returns in power and glory (Mk. 8:38). He gives them this glimpse in the transfiguration, where he is seen in his full glory and acknowledged by God as his beloved son to whom they must listen (Mk. 9:7).

1 2 WHO IS ELIJAH? (MK. 9:1 1-13)

In the last statement of the Old Testament, God promised that he would send Elijah the prophet again before the day of the Lord (Mal. 4:5-6). Elijah was a prophet in the eighth century bc, who lived out in the wilderness, wearing animal skins and a leather belt (2 Kgs. 1:8). When John the Baptist appeared, he came in a similar style (Mt. 3:4).

Jesus makes it clear that John was the fulfilment of the prophecy concerning Elijah. The indication, then, is that Elijah was the prototype forerunner figure, who would set a model for John, who himself would pave the way for Jesus.

1 3 WHAT DOES IT MEAN TO CUT OFF YOUR HAND, ETC? (MK. 9:43-48)

Jesus obviously did not intend that a Christian should physically cut off a hand or foot, or pluck out an eye. Jesus is using this dramatic form to make a point: 'If anything is stopping you from entering the kingdom of God, it is better to take drastic and perhaps even sacrificial action to rid yourself of that impediment, whatever it is, than to end up in hell for ever.'

The logic is obvious: **temporary pain is better than eternal punishment**.

1 4 WHAT DOES JESUS SAY ABOUT DIVORCE? (MK. 1 0:1 - 1 2)

Jesus is making it clear that divorce is always against the perfect purpose of God. God's plan, since creation, is that married people should live together for the whole of their lives (Mk. 10: 6-9, cf. Gen. 2:24). This is God's perfect plan.

Jesus also emphasised that if people seek a divorce because they have found an alternative partner, such action is adultery (Mk. 10:11-12). It is only because people's hearts are so hard (Mk. 10:5) that divorce could ever be permitted. The two-fold danger is either that we use the concession of verse 5 as an excuse for deliberate sin, or, alternatively, that we think of divorce as cutting us forever out of the will of God.

Christ came to die for all sin, including the failures of divorce. In talking to the Samaritan woman in John 4, Jesus knew that she had already been divorced five times

CHRISTIANITY
EXPLORED

and was now living with a sixth man. But even knowing these facts, he still freely offered her acceptance and forgiveness: 'If you knew the gift of God and who it is that asks you for a drink, you would have asked him and he would have given you living water' (Jn. 4:10).

It is not our role to be hard and judgmental. Like Jesus, we must freely hold out the water of forgiveness, cleansing and eternal life, while still pointing towards the high standard that God has permanently set for faithful marriage.

If the subject of divorce becomes a major issue in your **Christianity Explored** group, it may be advisable to arrange an extra session and involve a minister or counsellor who can explain the biblical position lovingly.

15 WHY DID JESUS CURSE THE FIG-TREE?

(MK. 11:12-14,20-25)

This action has perplexed many Christians as it was Jesus' only destructive miracle. Two suggestions can be made:

• Jesus was teaching his disciples about the power of prayer. Certainly that was the interpretation that he himself gave in the following verses (Mk. 11:22-24). Jesus was in effect saying, 'This power is available to you, too.'

• Many commentators have also suggested that this is an acted parable or a parable without words - a common device used by the Old Testament prophets. This incident is sandwiched between Jesus' two visits to the Temple. Although it should have been the most spiritual place on earth his first visit uncovers its spiritual bankruptcy and he returns the following day to cleanse the Temple (Mk. 11:15-19).

Some suggest that the fig-tree represents Israel and the Temple represents worship. Instead of finding spiritual fruitfulness in the Temple, he finds barrenness, like the fig-tree. Just as the fig-tree is cursed, so too Israel will come under God's curse and condemnation for her spiritual emptiness.

This idea of the coming destruction of the Temple is taken up more fully in chapter 13. This prophecy was fulfilled when the Temple and the city of Jerusalem were destroyed by the Roman armies in AD 70, about thirty seven years later.

16 WILL THERE BE MARRIAGE IN HEAVEN?
(MK. 12:18-27)

What is the point of this trick question? In Jesus' day there were two major religious parties: the Pharisees, who believed in life after death and the Sadducees, who said that death was the end and maintained there was no hope of life beyond the grave, or of resurrection (Mk. 12:18).

The Sadducees thus came up with this question and in his answer to them Jesus makes two points. Firstly, there is life beyond the grave but no marriage relationships, as such. This does not mean that married couples will not know each other in heaven - just that earthly relationships will have ended. Secondly, God did not say, 'I **was** the God of Abraham, Isaac, Jacob' but 'I **am** the God of Abraham'. I am still their God because they live on! The hope of the resurrection is the central Christian hope.

17 WHAT IS THE 'ABOMINATION THAT
CAUSES DESOLATION'? (MK. 13:14)

This is one case where the parallel passage in another Gospel gives us the key. Luke 21 is the parallel passage to Mark 13 and Luke has a tendency to explain difficult words or expressions in his Gospel.

In place of Mark 13:14, Luke has these words, 'When you see Jerusalem being surrounded by her armies ... then let those who are in Judea flee to the mountains' (Lk. 21:20-21).

Luke substitutes 'Jerusalem surrounded by her armies' for the word 'abomination'. In ad 65 the Roman armies surrounded Jerusalem after a political uprising. After a terrible five-year war, the Roman armies entered the city, desecrated the Holy of Holies in the temple, then proceeded to pull down both the Temple and the city. Jesus' words in Mark 13 came to pass.

CHRISTIANITY
EXPLORED

18 WHY DIDN'T JESUS KNOW THE DATE OF HIS OWN RETURN? (MK. 13:32)

Some people have suggested that because Jesus did not know the date of his own return, this means that he is less than perfect, less than divine. Since God is omniscient (knowing everything) Jesus cannot, therefore, be God. However, Jesus willed that he would only give the words that his Father gave him to know and teach (Jn. 14:24). The date of the second coming was not part of this teaching. Unlike Jesus, we find it impossible to control the thoughts that come into our thinking, but he would have had complete control over the gate of his human consciousness and could shut off those things that were not his mission to teach.

19 WAS THE DARKNESS AN ECLIPSE? (MK. 15:33)

It has been suggested that the darkness over the cross of Jesus was caused by a daytime eclipse of the sun, but this is not possible in astronomic terms. Jesus was crucified at the time of the Jewish Passover, which is always at full moon. At full moon, the heavenly bodies are in an almost straight line of sun - earth - moon. To have a daytime eclipse of the sun, the bodies must be in an exact straight line of sun - moon - earth.

We can truly say that **the darkness and the earthquake that marked Jesus' death** (Mt. 27:51) **indicated a shudder passing through nature at the death of the Son of God**.

20 WHY IS THERE AN ODD ENDING TO MARK'S GOSPEL? (MK. 16)

Most scholars agree that Mark's Gospel ends starkly at Mark 16:8. It is a brilliant ending, entirely in keeping with the abrupt way in which Mark begins his gospel with Jesus' baptism. Although the women have seen the empty tomb, and have been informed of the resurrection of Jesus, they nevertheless flee, 'trembling and bewildered' because, like Peter (who denies Christ three times in Mk. 14:66-72), they have not yet seen who Jesus is, why he came, and what it means to follow him. They are still partially blind, so they flee. This abrupt ending provokes the question, 'Have **you** seen who Jesus is yet - and that he has risen - or are you partially blind like these women and like Peter?' How is the cliff-hanger of verse 8 played out in **our** lives?

Verses 9-20 appear to be attempts by later writers to add a fuller resurrection ending to Mark. However, even the style of the Greek original changes after verse 8 and it is evident that the oldest manuscripts do not include this section. It is not part of Mark's original, thus we should treat it only as an interesting footnote.

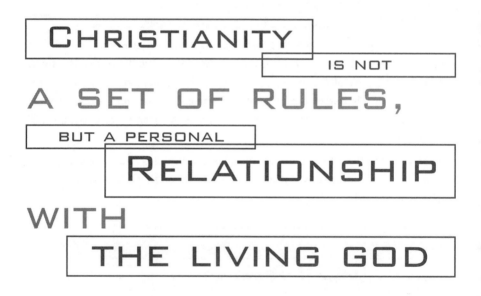

CHRISTIANITY IS NOT A SET OF RULES, BUT A PERSONAL RELATIONSHIP WITH THE LIVING GOD

CHRISTIANITY
EXPLORED

GUIDELINES ON LEADING BIBLE STUDIES

1 A CLEAR AIM

One of the essential skills of a Bible study leader is to have a clear vision of the main thing you want to achieve in your time together. **If you have no aim, you can be sure of accomplishing it!** Studies without a specific goal are rambling and incoherent. To have a different aim than the passage of Scripture is even more dangerous. Ask yourself the aim of the passage and what Mark intended when he wrote it. Your aim should be the same - to teach the main point of the passage in a way that people can understand. As you prepare your study, write down the goal and it will help you to ask questions in line with that.

2 GOOD QUESTIONS

It is a waste of time having a crystal-clear understanding of a passage but failing to communicate the main points in a study. It is critical to ask good questions which contribute to the aim of the study, by discovering:

- What the passage is saying, i.e. who is saying what to whom? When? Where?
- What the passage means, i.e. why does Mark include this incident? Why is it here? How does it follow on from what comes before? How does it set up what follows?
- How the passage should impact us, i.e. what is the main point of application? How does this incident change our view of Jesus? How should we respond to him?

In addition, good questions will:

- require some (but not too much) thought;
- give rise to discussion among the participants;
- make people look at the Bible and
- be clear and simple.

3 DEALING WITH ANSWERS

During the study discussions you will often get replies which approach the answer to a question, but are not complete. A key Bible study skill is to work out how you get from these initial answers to a better, more biblical answer. You should only be satisfied with a discussion that changes people's views in line with the aim of the study. Some key points to develop this:

- Don't be afraid to graciously correct a wrong answer, e.g. 'Thank you John, I'm not sure that's what's going on here.'

- Have further questions in mind to develop the initial answer, e.g. 'What did you mean by that?' 'What does everyone else think?' 'Where does it say that?'

- Have specific follow-on questions in mind for certain points, e.g. you could build on the study question of who Peter recognises Jesus to be and why this is important (Mk. 8:29) by asking how much the disciples have understood up to this point and how Jesus has reacted to their misunderstanding.

4 GROUP DYNAMICS

Our aim in these study times should be to have a discussion about a passage of Scripture in order to work out its meaning and its implications for us. Sometimes the group composition produces possible obstacles to effective Bible study, with personalities such as:

- 'Silent Susan' - best dealt with by encouraging people to work in groups of two or three at points during the study and then feeding back to the main group;

- 'Talkative Timothy' - depending on how well you know him, either introduce small group work to give others an opportunity to speak or have a quiet and tactful word;

- 'Pedestal Patrick' - where every answer comes back to the leader and there is no group discussion. Best dealt with by supplementary questions to facilitate group discussion.

5 APPLICATION

The result of Bible study should be transformed thinking and living. God warns us about the peril of ignoring his word (e.g. Jas. 1:22-24). You should, therefore, give time in the studies to considering the implications of a passage. It is worth bearing in mind that:

- often it is our understanding and attitudes that are wrong (with regard to God, his plan and ourselves). It is only once these are exposed and changed that our living can change;

- Mark's main application is clear from Mark 1:14-15 - we need to repent and believe. However, each week's study will give us a different emphasis - what do we need to turn from this week? What do we need to believe about Jesus in this study?

Participants will often only grasp the implications of a passage if you have put time into questions to draw out applications and spent time on your own thinking through how the passage should affect you personally.

FOLLOW UP

Christianity Explored is not designed to be a ten-week conveyor belt which either ships unbelievers into the Christian faith - or tips them off in the street outside. Once the course is over, the hard work for leaders is often just beginning. It is therefore vital to have a coherent follow-up strategy in place for all participants.

SELF-EVALUATION FORM

You may consider giving out a self-evaluation form to the course participants during the last week of *Christianity Explored*, a sample of which can be found in Appendix IV of *The Handbook*. This can be valuable in challenging course participants to think about where they are with Christ, and it can help direct their thoughts on future plans.

STAY IN TOUCH

Having spent ten weeks going through the **Christianity Explored** course with your group, you will undoubtedly have had some intimate discussions, and got to know individuals quite well. In these circumstances, it would be quite wrong simply to 'drop' group members once the course comes to an end. Whatever their response has been, God has not given up on them, and neither should you. Furthermore, if the friends who brought these people see a genuine interest maintained, they will feel more confident about bringing others along.

Plan to stay in touch with all the members of your group, and discuss it with your co-leaders so that each participant has at least one Christian taking a special interest in them.

ARRANGE FOLLOW UP FOR NEW BELIEVERS

If anyone in your group has made a commitment to Christ for the first time, praise the Lord! It's important for them to get some follow up so that a firm foundation of teaching, prayer, fellowship and service can be laid for the rest of their life. Invite them to start coming along to church with you if they're not already. It is often a difficult task to get people into the habit of meeting together regularly on a Sunday, but the concept of a Christian who doesn't go to church is foreign to the New Testament, so help them to take this seriously (Heb. 10:25). Be sure to take them along personally and introduce them to other Christians. Encourage them to become integrated within the church by joining a house group and finding an area of service within which they can participate.

ARRANGE FOLLOW UP FOR THOSE WHO HAVEN'T YET MADE A COMMITMENT

Don't be disheartened if some people have not made a commitment during the course. Bear in mind the parable of the growing seed in Mark 4:26-29, which shows that good things come to those who wait. Ask whether they would be interested in exploring Christianity further. If they are, one option is to invite them to come back and go through **Christianity Explored** again - some people have gone through the course three or four times before they felt ready to make a commitment.

CHRISTIANITY
E✝PLORED

Remember that they aren't just re-hearing the talks but re-reading **Mark's Gospel, which will work on their hearts each time it is opened**.

RECOMMEND OR GIVE AWAY GOOD BOOKS

Reading a good Christian book at the right time can be a hugely important step in a person's spiritual journey. Think carefully about the books you have read and see if there are any that would help the members of your group, whatever stage they are at. If you're not a big reader, ask around for advice about books suitable for people in different situations. The talk about the Bible on the Weekend Away is an opportunity to show options for Bible reading, such as daily notes and structured schedules for reading the Bible in a year.

READ THE BIBLE WITH SOMEONE

You may consider suggesting getting together with an individual on a regular basis to read through a book of the Bible and discuss what it means. This can be totally informal, just two friends with an open Bible trying to work out what it means. The intimacy and informality of this can provide a great context in which God speaks to both of you.

Questions to guide the study can be:

• What does the passage say?
• What does the passage mean within the context it's been written?
• What does the passage mean for me and how do I apply it in my life?

PRAY!

God longs for us to ask him for the things that are on our hearts. So continue to pray for all the members of the group, long after the course has come to an end. This is a supremely Christ-like way of caring for them. No-one sees us when we pray, but our Father in heaven hears the desires of our hearts and he promises to answer us when we pray in Jesus' name.

Pray for the growth, fruitfulness and joy of new believers. Pray for those who have not yet made a commitment, that the Lord will have mercy on them and send his Holy Spirit to open their blind eyes to see who Jesus is (2 Cor. 4:6). Pray for patience and wisdom for yourself as you wait for God's word to do its work.

This chapter includes the Study Guides for each week.

WEEKS 1-6

This includes:

• a summary of the talk you have just given;

• questions on a section of Mark's Gospel (The Big Picture) and the passage under consideration for the following week (Focus In), with suggested answers;

• a summary of the main points of the section of Mark's Gospel and notes on points of difficulty that may arise.

Don't worry if you don't have time to go through all of the questions – the most important thing is to listen to the participants and answer their questions about Christianity.

WEEKEND AWAY

There are four talks and two Bible studies. The second Bible study has a brief introduction, which the overall course leader gives.

WEEK 7

There are no Bible study questions this week. Instead, the material is intended to encourage participants to reflect on what they have heard about becoming a Christian. A summary of the talk and a copy of the prayer for participants to pray if they are ready to make a commitment to Jesus Christ is included here for the leader to use at the close of the discussion.

WEEKS 8-10

This includes a Bible study related to the talk, which leaders take participants through immediately afterwards. This is an opportunity for participants to learn how to get to grips with the passage with the help of their leaders.

STUDY GUIDES

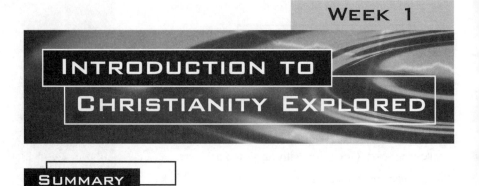

WEEK 1

INTRODUCTION TO CHRISTIANITY EXPLORED

SUMMARY

Introductory Question: If God were here and you could ask him one question, and you knew that he would answer it, what would it be?

There are lots of reasons why people ask questions about God. The wonder that we feel when we look at creation and the sense of despair that many people feel about life are just two of them.

Whatever questions we have about life and about God, we are unable to find the answers ourselves. We need God to break into our world and give them to us.

The Christian claim is that God has done exactly that in the person of Jesus Christ. Jesus stands at the heart of Christianity. The first verse of Mark's Gospel says: 'The beginning of the gospel about Jesus Christ, the Son of God.'

We need to see that Christianity is not primarily about rules, or religion; nor is it a matter of race – Christianity is great news about Jesus, and the possibility of knowing him personally.

Jesus meets the spiritual hunger so many feel, and the heart of this course is to have a one-to-one with Jesus Christ. Well over 1,000 years ago Augustine said, 'O God you have made us for yourself and our hearts are restless until they find their rest in you.'

So, where can you meet him? In the Bible. Mark asks each one of us to put his statement in Mark chapter 1, verse 1 to the test: is this really the beginning of the gospel (the great news) about Jesus Christ, the Son of God?

CHRISTIANITY
E✝PLORED

THE BIG PICTURE OF MARK'S GOSPEL

Please read Mark 1:1 – 3:6

The following questions are designed to assist you in reading this passage. Note any questions you may have or anything you find of particular interest in the space provided at the back of this booklet. There will be time for these to be discussed next week.

Summary: Jesus comes on the scene and begins to reveal who he is, but he is rejected by the authorities.

---

1 **In Mark 1:1-13, who points to Jesus? (Mark 1:2, 7, 11)**

   The Old Testament; John the Baptist; God the Father.

2 **Who is Jesus said to be?**

   All three say Jesus is special - he is the Lord whose way must be prepared; he is infinitely greater than John the Baptist, who is himself a great prophet; he is God's own Son.

3 **What sort of authority and power does Jesus exercise? (Mark 1:16-20, 21-27, 40-45; 2:1-12)**

   His authority when he calls people is such that they immediately drop what they are doing and follow him.

   His teaching has so much authority that it amazes people.

   He has authority over all sorts of evil spirits and sickness, even very serious illness.

   He even has authority to forgive sins.

4 **What has Jesus come to do? (Mark 1:14-15, 35-39; 2:17)**

   He has come to preach God's good news and to call people to believe in it.

   He has come to call those who are sinners - i.e. those who are rebelling against God.

5 **What sort of opposition does Jesus encounter? (Mark 1:12-14; 2:6-7,16,18; 3:2-6)**

   He faces opposition from the devil.

   Primarily, however, he faces opposition from the religious leaders who think he is blaspheming (i.e. being contemptuous of God) by claiming for himself authority that is only true of God. They don't like what he is doing and even this early in Jesus' ministry they want to kill him.

ADDITIONAL NOTES FOR LEADERS

MAIN POINTS OF THE PASSAGE

- Jesus demonstrates amazing power and authority;

- Jesus' priorities are to teach (Mk. 1:14-15, 35-39) and to restore outcasts to God by forgiving sin (Mk. 1:40 - 2:17);

- While many are amazed at this (Mk. 1:27-28; 2:12), the Jewish authorities become increasingly hostile (Mk. 2:7, 16, 24; 3:2) and want to kill Jesus (Mk. 3:6).

POSSIBLE POINTS OF DIFFICULTY

- **Mark 1:2-3** - Mark quotes from the Old Testament at the beginning of his book. He refers to Isaiah 40:3 and Malachi 3:1 which, in their context, promised that a messenger would come to announce the arrival of a rescuer King, the Christ, who would save the world before the day of judgement. The promise of a messenger is clearly fulfilled by John the Baptist in Mark 1:4-8. Even his clothing (Mk. 1:6) was like that of an Old Testament Prophet (Zech. 13:4) and, in particular, like Elijah (2 Kgs. 1:8; cf. Mal. 4:5).

- **'Pharisees'** - This group did not limit themselves to obeying the Old Testament Scriptures but adhered to a stricter tradition. They were thus regarded as among the most holy men in Israel. However, they viewed anyone who did not observe the same rigorous rules as a 'sinner' and an outcast (see Mk. 2:15-16).

- **'Bridegroom' (Mk. 2:19)** - Jesus is making the point that all fasting is totally inappropriate in his presence, just as it would be for wedding guests to mourn at a wedding. Jesus is identifying himself as the bridegroom of God's people promised in the Old Testament (Is. 54:5; 62:4-5; Hos. 2:16-20). As he came to deal with sin (Mk. 2:1-12) we should celebrate and sorrow is therefore inappropriate in his presence.

- **New cloth, new wine (Mk. 2:21-22)** - People were complaining that Jesus was not observing the religious rules and traditions of his day (Mk. 2:18). Jesus was saying that the faith that he had come to bring could not be 'fitted into' their legalistic religion. Jesus came to bring a living relationship with God; not rules or religious formulas but grace, love and peace.

- **'Sabbath' (Mk. 2:23)** - Sabbath means 'cease' or 'rest' and is derived from the Hebrew word used in Genesis 2:2 where God 'ceased' or 'rested' from his work of creation. It is therefore linked to the biblical concept of 'rest' whereby God's people

CHRISTIANITY
E*X*PLORED

dwell in God's place under God's gracious rule (Gen. 1 - 2). While this state of rest was lost at the Fall (Gen. 3), God promised to restore it to his people (Gen. 12:1-3; 17:8). The Sabbath was therefore an opportunity for God's people to remember both God's creation and his redemption of them (see Ex. 20:8-11; Deut. 5:12-15).

• **The disciples eat corn (Mk. 2:23-26)** - The Pharisees accused Jesus' followers of law-breaking; namely, 'reaping' on the Sabbath (Ex. 34:21). Jesus does not point out that what his disciples are doing can hardly be reaping. Instead, he rebukes the Pharisees for not remembering that Scripture failed to condemn David's act (1 Sam. 21:1-6). This narrow interpretation of the law by the Pharisees was not in accordance with Scripture.

• **'Herodians' (Mk. 3:6)** - These were loyal supporters of Herod Antipas, the puppet King of Judea, who depended on the controlling Roman Empire for his power. They would have seen Jesus as a threat to Herod's rule.

Focus In

In our time next week we will be looking in more detail at Mark 2:1–12. You may find it helpful to think about the following questions in advance of the next session.

---

1 What do people see as the world's greatest need?
Examples likely to include poverty, global warming, war, etc.

2 What is surprising about what Jesus says in Mark 2:5? What is the paralysed man's greatest need?
The man was lowered through the roof in order that he might be healed, not have his sins forgiven. Jesus' response shows that his greatest need is to have his sins forgiven, not be healed.

3 What is the significance of Jesus claiming to forgive the man's sin? (Mark 2:5-7)
Jesus is claiming to do that which only God can do, something the teachers of the law see clearly (Mk. 2:7).

4 What is the answer to Jesus' question in Mark 2:9? So why does he heal the paralytic? (Mark 2:9-12)
It is easier to say 'your sins are forgiven' because this cannot be verified, whereas healing the paralytic can be proven.
Jesus heals the man to show his power and authority and so to demonstrate that he can also do that which cannot be verified. Note the way that the paralytic does exactly what Jesus says (Mk. 2:12, cf. 2:9,11).

---

5 What does this incident show about who Jesus is? (Mark 2:7)

He is God, or at very least one to whom God has given his own power and authority, i.e. God's king on earth.

6 If you were a paralytic, what would you want Jesus to do for you? Why?

This question helps to provoke discussion. It should help participants to see the shock of Jesus' words in verse 5, i.e. do we see our sin as our greatest problem?

ADDITIONAL NOTES FOR LEADERS

This study introduces themes from the Week 2 talk on 'Jesus - who is he?' The key point is that Jesus has the authority to forgive sin (Mk. 2:10) and Jesus' words in Mark 2:5 have a shock impact. They expose the fact that our greatest need is not illness or paralysis but our sin; our rebellion against the God who made us. The religious authorities see the extent of Jesus' claim (Mk. 2:6-7). They consider it as blasphemous - a slander against God. God alone can forgive sin because God is the one against whom we rebel. Jesus is claiming divine authority. Either Jesus is a blasphemer or, if Jesus is God, the teachers of the law are slandering God!

Jesus refers to himself as the Son of Man (Mk. 2:10). If participants ask about this, it recalls Daniel 7:9-14 in which the 'son of man' was the name of a man who came to the Ancient of Days (Dan. 7:9,13), i.e. God, and was given authority to rule over all nations forever, starting from the last judgement (Dan. 7:14).

OTHER POSSIBLE QUESTIONS

• What is the source of Jesus' power?
• What is Jesus' priority in these verses?
• What does he mean?
• Why is that surprising?

You may choose to use these questions if you don't have time to go through the whole study and just want to ask one or two key questions to draw out the main points of the passage.

CHRISTIANITY
E⳨PLORED

JESUS - WHO IS HE?

SUMMARY

'Who is this?' the disciples asked, 'Even the wind and the waves obey him?' (Mark 4:41)

The disciples' question is a good one. When Jesus came into the world he demonstrated the power and authority of God himself everywhere he went. We have seen that Jesus has power and authority:

- to teach (Mark 1:21–22);
- over sickness (Mark 1:29–31);
- over nature (Mark 4:35–41);
- over life and death (Mark 5:35–42);
- to forgive sins (Mark 2:1–12).

Jesus claimed to be God on earth. It has been said he is the man you can't ignore. He is either a liar, a lunatic, or the Lord. And if he is the Lord, then it really is a scandal that we have made him a footnote in our lives.

THE BIG PICTURE OF MARK'S GOSPEL

Please read Mark 3:7 – 5:43

The following questions are designed to assist you in reading this passage. Note any questions you may have or anything you find of particular interest in the space provided at the back of this booklet. There will be time for these to be discussed next week.

Summary: Jesus gathers a people to whom he reveals more about who he is.

1 To whom is Jesus primarily teaching and revealing himself?
(Mark 3:13-19; 4:10-12, 33-41)

He is primarily teaching the disciples, particularly the twelve apostles.

2 Given Mark 3:6, why do you think Jesus concentrates on these people?

The religious establishment has rejected him and has already begun to seek his death, so Jesus seeks to gather and teach a new people.

3 What sort of authority and power do we see Jesus exercising?
(Mark 4:35-41; 5:1-20, 35-43)

He has power and authority over nature, even at its most violent.

He has power and authority over the most powerful evil spirits.

He has power and authority over the most intractable sickness.

He even has power and authority over death.

4 What does this add to what we saw of Jesus' power and authority in Mark 1:1 – 3:6?

We see Jesus' power and authority in areas we had not previously - e.g. over nature and death.

We see just how great his power and authority are - he has absolutely no difficulty in dealing with the worst, most hopeless and most insurmountable problems.

5 What does Jesus' authority and power teach us about who he is?

He exercises the power and authority that is God's, implying that he is God or at least God's king on earth.

6 What are the different ways in which people respond to Jesus?
(Mark 3:21-22; 4:40-41; 5:15-17, 27-28, 42)

His family think he is mad and the religious authorities think he's satanic.

The disciples are afraid.

The crowd who saw him heal a demon-possessed man are afraid and beg him to leave.

The sick woman trusts that Jesus can heal her.

Those who saw Jesus raise Jairus' daughter are astonished.

CHRISTIANITY
EXPLORED

ADDITIONAL NOTES FOR LEADERS

MAIN POINTS OF THE PASSAGE

• Jesus is rejected by many who question the sources of his authority (Mk. 3:20-35). In response to this and the religious authorities' desire to kill Jesus (Mk. 3:6), Jesus calls 12 apostles (i.e. messengers) to himself who become the focus of his teaching until the end of chapter 10.

• Opposition doesn't adversely affect Jesus' authority - it is even more striking in these chapters. He does things that only God can do, such as controlling the wind and waves (Mk. 4:35-41) and raising the dead (Mk. 5:35-42).

POSSIBLE POINTS OF DIFFICULTY

• **'Judea, Jerusalem, Idumea, etc' (Mk. 3:8)** - The places mentioned may be significant - they refer to the boundaries of the land originally allotted to Judah (Josh. 15), much of which was by Jesus' day inhabited by Gentiles (i.e. non-Jews).

• **The appointing of 12 apostles (Mk. 3:13-18)** - Jesus calls the 12 apostles on a mountainside. Significantly, God revealed himself to his people in the Old Testament on mountains (cf. Gen. 8, Ex. 19, and 1 Kgs. 18) and there had been 12 tribes of Israel (Gen. 49). Jesus is demonstrating that, as he is rejected by the old Israel (Mk. 2:18 - 3:6), so he calls a new Israel.

• **'He is possessed by Beelzebub' (Mk. 3:22)** - Having observed Jesus' miracles at first hand and noticed Jesus claiming to be God (Mk. 2:7), the teachers of the law have concluded that Jesus cannot be God and therefore must be satanic. Beelzebub is an old name for the devil. Note that the religious authorities did not question whether Jesus was powerful or whether the miracles had happened. Jesus replies that what they are suggesting is ludicrous - Satan cannot oppose Satan and be successful.

• **'Whoever blasphemes against the Holy Spirit will never be forgiven' (Mk. 3:29)** - As so often is the case in Bible study, the context here is the key. Jesus warns them that attributing his authority to evil (Mk. 3:22,30) is blasphemy because his authority comes from God. Jesus is the Son of Man with the authority to forgive sin (Mk. 2:10) and to reject him is to reject forgiveness. In other words, there is unlimited forgiveness (Mk. 3:28) unless the one who brings forgiveness, i.e. Jesus, is rejected. Such rejection is blasphemy, or slander, against the work of God's Spirit through the ministry of Jesus. It has nothing to do with swearing at the Holy Spirit - in simple terms it means to reject Jesus' offer of forgiveness continuously.

- **'Parables' (Mk. 4:2)** - These are a teaching device used by Jesus to convey spiritual truths. Jesus chooses to teach in parables, which have a clear surface meaning (often just one main point), but also a deeper meaning, which Jesus explains to those who listen (Mk. 4:1-34). There is a spiritual principle here - 'to those who have, more will be given'. The disciples were spiritually intrigued by the parables and drew nearer to Jesus to hear the explanation. However, to the unconcerned the parables just remained curious stories. They 'hear, but do not understand'.

- **Hearts being hardened (Mk. 4:11-12)** - This seems hard teaching. Parables divide people into two camps: all hear the parable (Mk. 4:1-8), all hear the call to listen (Mk. 4:9), but only some ask for explanation (Mk. 4:10). Their question reveals that they have been given the secret of the Kingdom. Jesus quotes Isaiah 6:9-10 in Mark 4:12. God told Isaiah that the result of his preaching would be that God would make those listening unable to understand. This appears unfair yet the phrase 'otherwise they might **turn** and be forgiven' tells us that those listening were facing away from God, having rejected him. Mark wants us to be clear that Jesus is judging those who have turned away except for those who, by grace, have been given the secret of the Kingdom of God.

FOCUS IN

In our time next week we will be looking in more detail at Mark 4:35–41. You may find it helpful to think about the following questions in advance of the next session:

1 **How do people respond to the claims of Jesus today? Why?**

   While some accept Jesus' claims, most reject them. They say that they lack evidence or they do not like the implications of Jesus being king.

2 **What is so remarkable about Jesus' calming of the storm?**

   The fact that Jesus instantly calmed not just the furious wind, but the huge waves as well - even though waves normally persist for hours or even days after the wind dies down - shows that a genuine miracle has taken place.

   His ability to accomplish this miracle with a simple word displays the extent of Jesus' power and authority - even a miracle of this magnitude is simple for him.

   The Old Testament is clear that only God has power and authority over wind and waves (Ps. 89:9).

CHRISTIANITY
E✝PLORED

3 What is the disciples' response to the situation they face in the boat *before* Jesus is woken up? Why are they responding in this way?
They are afraid because the storm is beyond their control, even though they are experienced fishermen, and they think they are going to die.
They do not realise that Jesus is more than capable of dealing with the storm because they do not yet realise who he is.

4 What is the disciples' response to what Jesus does and why do they respond in this way?
They are still terrified but for a different reason - they are beginning to see that Jesus is far greater and more powerful than they had previously thought and being in the presence of such awesome authority and power is frightening. However, they do not yet believe that Jesus is God's king, wielding God's power and authority.

5 How would you answer the disciples' question in Mark 4:41: 'Who is this? Even the wind and the waves obey him?' How should you respond to Jesus?
This question is designed to reveal whether the participants have grasped that Jesus is doing what only God can do. We should respond with belief and dependence rather than the fear shown by the disciples.

ADDITIONAL NOTES FOR LEADERS

This study recaps the main points from the Week 2 talk on 'Jesus - who is he?' The main point is that the disciples fail to recognise that Jesus is God caring for them. They therefore express terror rather than faith both before **and** after Jesus acts. Jesus is right to be angry with them in verse 40. Despite all the evidence of chapters 1-4, the disciples doubt Jesus' teaching in chapter 4 that his word is powerful. Having told the disciples to cross the lake he is not going to allow them to die on the way, but they don't believe him (Mk 4:38).

OTHER POSSIBLE QUESTIONS

• Why was it a desperate situation?
• What evidence is there that a miracle has occurred?
• Why is Jesus angry with them in Mark 4:40?

You may choose to use these questions if you don't have time to discuss the whole study and just want to ask one or two key questions to draw out the main points of the passage.

JESUS
- WHY DID HE COME?

SUMMARY

'I have not come to call the righteous, but sinners.' (Mark 2:17)

Jesus says that he came to earth to rescue rebels; he assumes that we are rebels who are in need of rescue.

When we look at the world, we have to admit that it is not the place that it should be. And when we are honest, we know that we are not the people we should be. We are far more wicked than we ever realised.

Someone asked Jesus what the greatest commandment was. He replied, 'Love the Lord your God with all your heart and with all your soul and with all your mind and with all your strength.' (Mark 12:30)

Our greatest crime is that none of us have loved God in that way. We have rebelled against him, taking the crown off his head and putting it firmly on our own.

We are more guilty than we ever realised. That is why we need Jesus to rescue us. But do we feel that need of rescue? As the Titanic sank, many of the passengers thought they weren't in danger, but that wasn't reality. In fact they were perishing, though they did not know it. So what is reality when it comes to our need of rescue? How dangerous do you think Jesus' warning in Mark 9:42-47 really is?

The great news is that Jesus came to rescue rebels just like us. Next week, we will explore just how he did it.

WE'RE MORE WICKED THAN WE EVER REALISED

BUT MORE LOVED THAN WE EVER DREAMED

CHRISTIANITY
EXPLORED

THE BIG PICTURE OF MARK'S GOSPEL

Please read Mark 6:1 – 8:29

The following questions are designed to assist you in reading this passage. Note any questions you may have or anything you find of particular interest in the space provided at the back of this booklet. There will be time for these to be discussed next week.

Summary: Jesus reveals the problem that he has come to deal with and his disciples eventually understand who he is.

---

1 **What does this passage add to what we've seen of Jesus' power and authority in chapters 1–5? (Mark 6:32-56; 7:31-37; 8:1-10, 22-26)**

   Jesus is able to meet the needs of the people, even when this involves creating vast amounts of food from nothing, so showing that he is God's shepherd. (See possible points of difficulty.) Jesus has the power and authority even to heal those who are completely blind and deaf.

2 **How are people responding to Jesus as they see his power and authority? (Mark 6:1-6, 14-16, 51-56; 7:37; 8:11)**

   Many are utterly amazed at what he is doing and are speculating wildly about who he is, but no one seems to be anywhere near the right answer.

   Others, however, are suspicious and offended at what they see.

3 **According to Jesus, what is the real need of the people? (Mark 6:34; 7:14-23)**

   They (and we) are like sheep without a shepherd, helpless and in need.

   They (and we) have hearts that are full of evil - this means that at the deepest, most unalterable level they (and we) are 'unclean', i.e. unacceptable to God.

4 **In most of the passage, how much do the disciples understand of who Jesus is and what he is saying? (Mark 6:36-37, 48-52; 7:17-18; 8:4, 14-21)**

   They don't understand who Jesus is, what he can do or what he is saying.

ADDITIONAL NOTES FOR LEADERS

MAIN POINTS OF THE PASSAGE

- Jesus reveals that preaching the gospel will meet rejection because of people's sin and people's failure to repent (Mk. 6:1-30).

- Jesus has come to rescue God's people. Mark draws on several Old Testament promises given to God's people at the time of the exile, seven hundred years before Jesus. As punishment by God for their rebellion at that time, the people of Israel were conquered by Assyria and Babylon and carried off to exile. God promised that the exile was not the end but that God would one day come to rescue his people. Thus, God's people looked forward to their Messiah, whose job was to rescue them and rule over them. (See points of difficulty below.)

- Rejection of the gospel by the religious authorities, the people of Jesus' home town, Herod, and others, and the misunderstanding of the disciples (Mk. 6:49-52) is caused by our unclean evil hearts (Mk. 7:18-23). Religion cannot help (Mk. 7:1-16). What is needed is a miracle (Mk. 8:22-30).

- Jesus reveals that he is the rescuer king of Gentiles as well as Jews (Mk. 7:24-30; 8:1-10) and brings the exile to an end by a miracle (Mk. 7:31-37 cf. Isaiah 35:5). Jesus is indeed the Christ (Mk. 8:29) but even the most privileged can only see that by a miracle (Mk. 8:22-30).

POSSIBLE POINTS OF DIFFICULTY

- **'He could not do any miracles there...' (Mk. 6:5)** - This cannot mean that the lack of faith demonstrated by Jesus' home town limited Jesus' power, as this would be inconsistent with Mark 3:6-11 and 4:35 - 5:20. Rather, those who reject the revelation they are given will receive no more (see Mk. 4:25 cf. 8:11-12).

- **Jesus sends out the Twelve (Mk. 6:7-11)** - Jesus sends out the 12 apostles telling them to expect some to accept and some to reject the gospel (Mk. 6:10-11). They are to reject those who, by refusing to listen, reject them. The reference to shaking off dust refers to an act by pious Jews on returning to Israel from Gentile countries. For the disciples to do it in a Jewish village was akin to calling the village Gentile!

- **John the Baptist (Mk. 6:14-29)** - Mark inserts this account of the death of John the Baptist into the account of the ministry of the Twelve to make an important point (Mk. 6:7-13, 30). It answers the implied question of Mark 6:1-13, i.e. why don't people see who Jesus is? Jesus is rejected because people, like Herod, will not repent, i.e. turn from their rebellion against God.

CHRISTIANITY
EXPLORED

- **'...like sheep without a shepherd' (Mk. 6:34)** - In Ezekiel 34, Israel is described as being like sheep without a shepherd because her leaders had not done their job properly (Ezek.34:1-6). Further, God promised to come himself to rescue his people (Ezek. 34:16) and shepherd them through his Messiah (Ezek. 34:23). Jesus is that rescuer, acting as God's shepherd by feeding the sheep in a clearly supernatural way (Mk. 6:30-44; 8:1-10), as God himself had done when rescuing Israel from Egypt (Ex. 16:32-35). Jesus is also said to 'pass by' the disciples as he walks on water in language reminiscent of God passing by Moses at the time he received the stone tablets. (Mk 6:48 cf. Ex 34:1-9) The fact that Jesus is God himself come to rescue is further affirmed by his announcement in Mark 6:50, 'Don't be afraid, I am' (cf. Exodus 3:14).

- **Syro-Phoenician woman (Mk. 7:24-30)** - Mark records this incident in order for us to see that the rescue Jesus brings is also for the Gentiles. The key to this passage lies in the fact that the woman was not a Jewess but a Gentile from near the city of Tyre. She sees that while the Jews come first, the Gentiles are also included. The children in the analogy refer to the Jews, while 'dogs' was an unflattering term used by Jews to describe the Gentiles. It should, therefore, come as no surprise to see Jesus doing a feeding miracle in a Gentile area (Mk. 8:1-10) for he is the rescuer of Jews and Gentiles.

- **The deaf and mute man (Mk. 7:31-37)** - You will recall, in Mark 4:11-12, that Mark quoted Isaiah 6:9-12 where Israel is described as blind and deaf. However, God promised that when he rescued his people he would open blind eyes and unstop deaf ears (Is. 35:5). Not only does Jesus heal a deaf and mute man, he also heals a blind man (Mk. 8:22-25). Jesus is indeed the Messiah and we, because of our evil hearts, need a miracle to be rescued. Both these miracles appear difficult to accomplish. This shows that something significant is happening and indicates how difficult it is to open eyes which are spiritually blind and ears which are spiritually deaf.

- **'...the yeast of the Pharisees and that of Herod' (Mk. 8:15)** - 'Yeast' means 'influence'. Just as a tiny amount of yeast has a significant effect on the whole batch of dough, so Jesus warns against the 'influence' of the Pharisees and Herod. Jesus is warning the disciples that, because they misunderstand who he is, there is a danger that they could become like the Pharisees and Herod (Mk. 8:11-13) and end up ultimately rejecting him. They are in a dangerous position because they are blind and deaf to who Jesus is, despite the clear evidence that he is the rescuer promised in the Old Testament (Mk. 6:30-44; 8:1-10).

In our time next week we will be looking in more detail at Mark 8:17–29. You may find it helpful to think about the following questions in advance of the next session:

1 **Who do people believe Jesus to be? On what do they base their views?**

Answers are likely to include a good teacher, wise guru, the first communist, etc. These views are based on preconceptions from Sunday school, Religious Education, etc.

2 **In Mark 8:29, who does Peter recognise Jesus to be and why is this important?**

Peter sees that Jesus is the Christ.

This is important because no-one so far has grasped this, despite all that Jesus has revealed of himself. The issue of recognising Jesus' identity has become increasingly important as the Gospel has gone on.

3 **What is surprising about the miracle Jesus performs in Mark 8:22-25?**

It seems surprisingly difficult to accomplish compared to other miracles which we would expect to be much harder but Jesus performs with ease.

4 **What do you think is the significance of the miracle, coming as it does between Mark 8:17-21 and Mark 8:27-29? How have the disciples come to understand who Jesus is?**

In Mark 8:17-21 the disciples do not see or understand who Jesus is, but in Mark 8:27-29 they have finally grasped his identity. The disciples have come to see who Jesus is by means of a miracle, just as the blind man saw by means of a miracle. The fact that Jesus appears to find this healing particularly difficult shows us how hard it is to heal the spiritually blind.

5 **In Mark 8:29, Jesus asks: 'But what about you? Who do you say I am?' How would you answer?**

This is designed to reveal where the participants stand with Christ.

CHRISTIANITY
EXPLORED

The main point of this study is that Jesus is the 'Christ'. In other words, Jesus is the long awaited Messiah, or king of God's people, and that the disciples only come to recognise this because of a miracle.

The miracle is sandwiched between the misunderstanding of the disciples in Mark 8:17-21 and their recognition in Mark 8:29. The 'difficulty' experienced by Jesus in healing the blind man (Mk. 8:23-25) is not meant to suggest that Jesus was running out of power or that the blind man did not have sufficient faith! We already know that Jesus works without people having faith (Mk. 4:35-41). Mark is seeking to prepare us for Peter's 'partial' sight. When Peter announces that Jesus is the Christ in Mark 8:29 he is like the man in Mark 8:24, i.e. he has partial sight. It is clear from the verses that follow that he has not yet realised why Jesus has come (Mk. 8:30-33).

OTHER POSSIBLE QUESTIONS

- What has changed in Peter between Mark 8:21 and Mark 8:29?
- How has this happened?

You may choose to use these questions if you don't have time to discuss the whole study and just want to ask one or two key questions to draw out the main points of the passage.

THE GREAT NEWS IS THAT JESUS CAME TO RESCUE REBELS JUST LIKE US

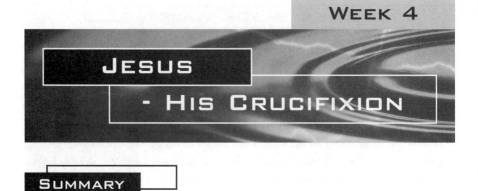

JESUS
- HIS CRUCIFIXION

SUMMARY

'For even the Son of Man did not come to be served, but to serve, and to give his life as a ransom for many.' (Mark 10:45)

The cross stands right at the heart of the Christian faith. That is a surprise because the cross is a symbol of execution. So, why is it so precious to Christians, when it was such a horrific means of execution? It can only be because of what happened on the cross.

Mark's account of the death of Jesus in Mark 15:16–39 explains what was happening as Jesus died.

GOD IS ANGRY ... AT JESUS, NOT US!

MARK 15:33

The darkness tells us that God is acting to punish rebellion against him. However, his anger is not poured out on us who deserve it, but on Jesus as he dies.

JESUS IS ABANDONED ... IN OUR PLACE

MARK 15:34

On the cross, Jesus suffered great spiritual agony. He was abandoned by God; punished so that we could go free. He died as a substitute for those people who trust in him. He was being forsaken by God, so that we need never be.

CHRISTIANITY
EXPLORED

WE CAN BE ACCEPTED ... BECAUSE JESUS DIED

MARK 15:37-39

The tearing from top to bottom of the temple curtain, which separated God's people from coming into his presence in the Holy of Holies, symbolises the end of the need for this massive barrier. Jesus' death means that there is now nothing to prevent me from having a friendship with God because my sin has been paid for. Because the curtain was torn in two, we can know for sure that we are accepted by God.

While it's true that we're more wicked than we ever realised, the cross tells us that we are more loved than we ever dreamed. We therefore face a clear choice: to take our rebellion to the grave and face Jesus in judgement, or to take our rebellion to the cross of Jesus and face Jesus as our Saviour.

How did the people around the cross respond to it? We see the responses of:

• the busy soldiers (Mark 15:24);
• the self-satisfied religious (Mark 15:31);
• Pilate the coward (Mark 15:15);
• the bystander (Mark 15:35–36);
• the Roman centurion (Mark 15:39).

Can you identify with any of these responses?

THE BIG PICTURE OF MARK'S GOSPEL

Please read Mark 8:30 – 10:52

The following questions are designed to assist you in reading this passage. Note any questions you may have or anything you find of particular interest in the space provided at the back of this booklet. There will be time to discuss these next week.

Summary: Jesus reveals to the disciples what he has come to do and what it means to follow him.

1 **Jesus gives himself the title Son of Man in Mark 8:31, 9:9, and 9:31. What do we learn about the identity of the Son of Man from Mark 8:38 and 9:2-9? (See also Daniel 7:9-14.)**

He will come in the Father's glory and we are not to be ashamed of his words (Mk. 8:38).

He is greater than Elijah and Moses (Mk. 9:2-9).

He is God's Son and to whom the disciples are told to listen to him (Mk. 9:7).

He is given authority to rule an everlasting kingdom, starting from the final judgement (Dan. 7:14).

2 **What 'must' and 'will' the Son of Man do, according to Mark 8:31, 9:31 and 10:33-34?**

He must suffer, be rejected by the religious leaders, be killed and, three days later, rise again.

He will be betrayed.

He will be handed over to the Romans by the religious leaders in Jerusalem.

He will be mocked, spat on, flogged and killed.

3 **How can we reconcile this with what we see of the Son of Man in Mark 8:38, 9:7 and Daniel 7:9-14?**

In this world Jesus must suffer and die as a ransom for his people (Mk. 10:45) but he will return in his Father's glory at the end of time, when he comes again (Mk. 8:38).

It is at the end of time that Jesus will be seen to be the great and glorious king, as he is given glory and authority to rule forever.

4 **What must anyone who wants to be a follower of Jesus do and why must they do this? (Mark 8:34-38)**

They must deny themselves, take up their cross and follow Jesus (Mk. 8:34).

It is the only thing to do in the light of who Jesus is and why he has come (Mk. 8:27-31).

Leaders should not be tempted to soften the cost of following Jesus.

It is the only way of saving their life in eternity (Mk. 8:35-38), i.e. the cost of not following Jesus is much greater.

CHRISTIANITY
EXPLORED

5 To what extent do the disciples understand what Jesus must do and what it means to follow him? Why does this matter? (Mark 8:32-33; 9:31-35; 10:32-45; cf. 8:35-38)

They do not understand that Jesus must suffer and die (Mk. 8:32-38).

They think his kingdom is about greatness rather than service (Mk. 9:31-35).

They do not understand that only Jesus can die to ransom many (Mk. 10:32-45).

Unless they understand these things they will not be prepared to give up all to follow Jesus (Mk. 8:35-38).

6 What is going to be the solution to their lack of understanding? (Mark 10:46-52)

They need a miracle to enable them to see their own need for mercy and the reason why Jesus has come (Mk. 10:46-52), in much the same way that they need a miracle to see who Jesus is (cf. Mk. 8:22-29).

ADDITIONAL NOTES FOR LEADERS

MAIN POINTS OF THE PASSAGE

- Jesus reveals that he is the Son of Man, i.e. the one with all authority who rules over the world forever, starting from the final judgement (see Dan. 7:9-14). Further, in the transfiguration (Mk. 9:2-8), Jesus appeared like God himself and was referred to as 'Son' by God himself.

- However, the Son of Man must suffer and die because humankind cannot save itself (Mk. 9:14-29, 42-50; cf. 7:20-23; 10:17-27) and therefore needs to be ransomed (Mk. 10:45).

- Following Jesus involves going the way that Jesus went, i.e. suffering and serving (Mk. 8:34-38; 9:33-41; 10:42-45).

- However, the disciples fail to grasp much of this teaching (Mk. 8:31-32; 9:10-11, 28, 32-41; 10:32-41).

- **'Get behind me Satan' (Mk. 8:32-33)** - Peter had recognised that Jesus was the Christ, God's king in God's world, but he could not understand why God's king must die as Jesus predicted (v. 31). However, Jesus' rebuke of Peter teaches us how central the cross is to Jesus' mission. What Jesus was saying was radically new; they were not prepared for a rejected Messiah. The fact that the other disciples were present called for a strong and open rebuke by Jesus. To reject God's plan that the Messiah should endure the cross was nothing less than a temptation from Satan himself.

- **'will not taste death before they see the kingdom of God come with power' (Mk. 9:1)** - this is likely to refer to the transfiguration of Jesus in Mark 9:2-10. Jesus has been revealing that he is the Son of Man who will rule in eternity, but who will suffer and die in this world (Mk. 8:31-38). However, in order to confirm his disciples' new understanding that he is the Christ (Mk. 8:29), Jesus promises them a dress rehearsal of what he will be like when he returns in power and glory (Mk. 8:38). He gives them this glimpse in the transfiguration: Jesus' divine power and glory is revealed (Mk. 9:2b-4) and he is acknowledged by God as his son, to whom they must listen (Mk. 9:7).

- **'Elijah and Moses' (Mk. 9:4)** - both of these represent the Old Testament: Moses represents the law and Elijah (a prophet in the eighth century BC) represents the Prophets. The fact that they talk with Jesus demonstrates that he is the one to whom the Old Testament bears witness, i.e. God's promised king. Later, in Mark 9:11-13, it is clear that the disciples have failed to recognise that John the Baptist was the Elijah-like messenger promised in Malachi 4:5-6.

- **'This kind can come out only by prayer' (Mk. 9:29)** - this is a notoriously difficult passage. The context of the passage, as always, is the key. Jesus predicts his death on the cross three times in chapters 8-10 (Mk. 8:31; 9:31; 10:33-34). His teaching in these chapters explains why the cross is necessary. This incident further displays the necessity of the cross, because all of humanity is bound in sin and requires the power that Jesus alone has to be rescued. Given the fact that the disciples had been delegated authority over evil spirits in Mark 6:7, what Jesus seems to be saying is that this miracle requires power that only he has. The boy is a picture of human captivity to sin; the boy is only healed when his father cries out to Jesus in Mark 9:24, 'Help me overcome my unbelief.' In other words, it only happens when the father asks God through prayer to do that which he alone can do, and recognises that he does not deserve God to do it.

CHRISTIANITY
E✝PLORED

- **The horror of hell (Mk. 9:42-50)** - Jesus warns so strongly against seeking to be great (Mk. 9:33-37) because it is self-centred, rejects the cross, and leads to the sin of destroying the faith of other Christians. Sin is serious because it leads to hell, which is so terrible that we should take drastic action to avoid it. Jesus obviously did not intend that a Christian should physically cut off a hand or foot, or pluck out an eye. Indeed, it must be remembered, as Jesus taught in Mark 7:18-23, that our problem is not our hand, or foot or eye - but our heart. We are therefore helpless and need rescue.

- **'receive the kingdom of God like a little child' (Mk. 10:15)** - Jesus is calling on the disciples to realise that they have nothing to offer and must therefore depend fully on God. The phrase does not mean they should be innocent or humble - neither of which are traits of most children!

- **'Can you drink the cup I drink...' (Mk. 10:38)** - Jesus is referring to the cup of God's wrath (Jer. 25:15-16) and showing that the disciples don't know what they are talking about. They, unlike Jesus, have their own sin to deal with and therefore cannot take God's wrath for other people - an innocent and willing substitute is required. Jesus is such a substitute.

- **'Jesus, Son of David, have mercy on me' (Mk. 10:47)** - The contrast between Bartimaeus and the disciples is stark: they treat Jesus as a teacher (Mk. 10:35) while Bartimaeus recognises who Jesus is - the promised king. The disciples ask for glory (Mk. 10:35-37) but he asks for mercy; they want thrones while he wants to see (Mk. 10:51). Ironically, he is the one who can see what is truly important - he recognises who Jesus is while the disciples are spiritually blind.

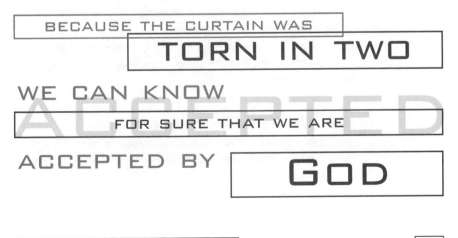

BECAUSE THE CURTAIN WAS

TORN IN TWO

WE CAN KNOW

FOR SURE THAT WE ARE

ACCEPTED BY GOD

In our time next week we will be looking in more detail at Mark 10:17–34. You may find it helpful to think about the following questions in advance of the next session.

1 **What things prevent people following Jesus?**

   Examples may include family, relationships, career, ambitions, the need to change, time, etc.

2 **What prevented the man following Jesus? Why did this matter? (Mark 10:17-22; 8:35-37)**

   While he believed he had kept the commandments, he was unwilling to give up his wealth, which implied that he was not treating God as God.

   Jesus had already warned of the danger of gaining the whole world at the expense of one's soul (Mk. 8:36). This man is in danger of forfeiting his soul.

3 **What point is Jesus making when he refers to the camel in Mark 10:24-25? According to Mark 10:26-27, who can be saved?**

   It is impossible for the rich to enter the kingdom of God without first recognising Jesus. Since in that culture they were considered to be blessed by God and would have the most chance of getting to heaven, this shows that no-one can claim this destiny in their own right.

   Salvation is only possible with God.

4 **What does Mark 10:32-34 tell us about how God accomplishes salvation (cf. Mark 10:45)? What then is the answer to the man's question in Mark 10:17?**

   God's means of salvation is the cross; it is the only way to ransom people. Humankind cannot do anything to inherit eternal life; only Jesus can obtain it for us by dying on the cross.

5 **What are the issues preventing you from following Jesus?**

   This question is designed to reveal what is stopping people turning to Jesus. It may be that you tackle this in conversations with individuals rather than ask the group as a whole.

CHRISTIANITY
EXPLORED

ADDITIONAL NOTES FOR LEADERS

This study recaps on the need for the cross, as highlighted in the Week 4 talk, and introduces themes from Week 5 on Jesus' gift of grace. The main point of the study passage is that it is impossible for anyone to do anything to gain eternal life (Mk. 10:26-27; cf. 10:17). Instead, salvation is only possible with God (Mk. 10:27) and God's means of salvation is by Jesus' death on the cross (Mk. 10:32-34).

In contrast to the little children in Mark 10:13-16, this rich man would have every reason to enter the Kingdom of God in the eyes of the Pharisees. However, unlike the children, he slinks away (Mk. 10:22). He clearly respected Jesus, was concerned about eternal life (Mk. 10:17), was morally upright since his childhood (Mk. 10:20), and was wealthy - considered a sign of God's blessing.

His key problem is thinking he can **do** something to gain eternal life (Mk. 10:17). Jesus exposes his misunderstanding by first reminding him that only God is good. This alone ought to have made him realise he was morally bankrupt. Secondly, Jesus quotes the second half of the Ten Commandments, which should have caused the man to recognise his failure to keep the first five, including not to have any other gods. Finally, Jesus shows the man the identity of his idol - his wealth (Mk. 10:21). Jesus warns the man to follow him in this world in order to gain treasure in heaven (Mk. 10:21 cf. Mk. 8:34-38). It is an act of love for Jesus to tell the man exactly what he most needs to hear.

Peter claims that the disciples have done what the rich man had not done (Mk. 10:28; cf. 10:21; 1:18,20). However, Jesus rebukes Peter for assuming God can be in anyone's debt. It is not a prosperity gospel - there will be persecutions (Mk. 10:30) - but it is a gospel of grace. Jesus wanted the rich man and the disciples to see that they could not save themselves. He wanted them to see that the cross is vital.

OTHER POSSIBLE QUESTIONS

- Why is the man's question promising? (Mk. 10:17)
- How does Jesus expose the man's problem?
- In what way does Peter misunderstand what Jesus has been saying? (Mk. 10:28-31)
- How does Jesus correct him?

You may choose to use these questions if you don't have time to discuss the whole study and just want to ask one or two key questions to draw out the main points of the passage.

JESUS
- HIS GIFT OF GRACE

SUMMARY

If you were to die tonight and found yourself standing before God, and he asked, 'Why should I let you into my heaven?', what would you reply?

The wrong answer: *What I have done*

God, you should accept me because I have:

- Lived a good life;
- Kept the Ten Commandments;
- Given to charity;
- Prayed and read the Bible;
- Been to church;
- Been baptised.

If we are trusting in the things we have done, God will not allow us into his heaven. We are too wicked to make it to heaven by our own efforts - see Mark 7:20–23.

The right answer: *What Christ has done*

God, you should accept me because of what Christ has done for me, and that alone. Read Ephesians 2:8–10.

If we are trusting in what Jesus has done, by dying on the cross for us, God will welcome us into his heaven with open arms.

NOT

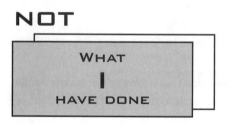

WHAT
I
HAVE DONE

BUT

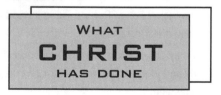

WHAT
CHRIST
HAS DONE

CHRISTIANITY
EXPLORED

God's love for us is unconditional. We could never earn it. There is nothing we can do to make God love us more and nothing we can do to make him love us less. Jesus has done everything that needs to be done to get us to heaven.

Forgiveness and eternal life are the free gifts of God to all who will receive the giver – that is Jesus Christ. And finding my identity in God's grace makes the Christian life a life of joy and gratitude. So, we're more wicked that we ever realised but more loved than we ever dreamed.

THE BIG PICTURE OF MARK'S GOSPEL

Please read Mark 11:1 – 13:37

The following questions are designed to assist you in reading this passage. Note any questions you may have or anything you find of particular interest in the space provided at the back of this booklet. There will be time for these to be discussed next week.

Summary: Jesus goes to Jerusalem to confront the Jewish authorities and to judge man-centred religion.

1 **How do the crowds treat Jesus as he arrives in Jerusalem? (Mark 11:1-10)**

The crowds proclaim Jesus as the Messiah, or the long-promised king.

2 **What is the significance of the detail in Mark 11:1-10? (see Zechariah 9:9)**

Jesus is in control of events.

Jesus is the promised king.

3 **How do the Jewish authorities treat Jesus? (Mark 11:27-33; 12:13-17)**

They question Jesus' authority and seek to trap him with trick questions.

They deal dishonestly with the facts.

They look for an opportunity to arrest Jesus and kill him.

4 **What does Jesus say will happen to the Jewish authorities in Mark 12:1-12?**

As the tenants in the parable were to be killed for their rebellion against the vineyard owner and the vineyard given to others, so the Jewish authorities will be rejected by God and will no longer be his people.

5 How does Jesus describe the period before the end of the world? (Mark 13:5-13)

A time of upheaval and many disasters.

A time of deception, with many claiming to be the Christ.

A time of persecution for Jesus' followers.

6 How should the followers of Jesus act while they wait for the end? (Mark 13:9-13, 32-37)

Be on their guard for false signs.

Be alert, living in the knowledge that the end will come.

Preach the gospel.

ADDITIONAL NOTES FOR LEADERS

MAIN POINTS OF THE PASSAGE

- Jesus enters Jerusalem, acknowledged as king (Mk. 11:1-10), to collect the allegiance that is rightly his as the Son of God (Mk. 12:1-6,17).

- Jesus passes judgement on Israel's religion (Mk. 11:12-33), as it makes them refuse to worship God.

- God will judge them for such rejection (Mk. 12:7-12; 13:1-2).

POSSIBLE POINTS OF DIFFICULTY

- **Jesus curses the fig-tree (Mark 11:12-14, 20-25)** - Mark interleaves the cursing of the fig-tree with the events in the temple (Mk. 11:15-19, 27-33). In the same way that Jesus curses the fig-tree for fruitlessness, he judges Israel's man-centred and barren religion as symbolised by the temple. Indeed, the temple and the city of Jerusalem were destroyed by the Roman armies in AD 70.

- **One bride for seven brothers? (Mk. 12:18-27)** - In Jesus' day there were two major religious parties: the Pharisees, who believed in life after death and the Sadducees, who said that death was the end. To them there was no hope of life beyond the grave, or of resurrection (Mk. 12:18). The Sadducees thus came up with this question (Mk. 12:18-23). In his answer to them, in Mark 12:24-27, Jesus says two things. First, there is life beyond the grave but no married relationships, as such. This does not mean that married couples will not know each other in heaven

CHRISTIANITY
EXPLORED

- just that earthly relationships will have ended. Secondly, God is still the God of Abraham, Isaac and Jacob because they live on. A central hope of Christianity is the certain expectation of resurrection.

- **The 'abomination that causes desolation' (Mk. 13:14)** - The parallel passage in Luke describes 'Jerusalem surrounded by her armies', and is thus seen as referring to the occasion in AD 65 when Roman armies surrounded Jerusalem after a political uprising. After a horrific five-year conflict, the Roman armies entered the city, desecrated the Holy of Holies in the temple, then proceeded to pull down the temple and destroy the city. Thus Jesus' words in Mark 13 came to pass.

- **The lesson from the fig-tree (Mk. 13:28-31)** - the lesson we are to learn from the fig-tree is that just as buds on a fig-tree suggest summer is near, so a certain event suggests that the end is near. The event in Jesus' mind is the destruction of the temple and Jerusalem in AD 70 (Mk. 13:14-23). This seems clear from Mark 13:24 where Jesus explains what will happen 'in those days, following that distress'. In other words, when Jerusalem and the temple have been destroyed, nothing else is left to happen before the end of the world comes.

FOCUS IN

In our time next week we will be looking in more detail at Mark 12:1–12. You may find it helpful to think about the following questions in advance of the next session.

> **1 To whom does Jesus tell this parable? (Mark 12:1 cf. 11:27, 33)**
>
> The religious authorities who have just been questioning his authority in Mark 11:27-33.
>
> **2 What is the crime of the tenants in the parable? What does their behaviour in Mark 12:1-8 suggest they think of the owner?**
>
> They did not give the owner what was due to him, i.e. the fruit of the harvest.
>
> They thought the owner would not mind his servants being killed and that he would not act in response to his own son being killed.
>
> **3 Why is Jesus' description of the son significant? (Mark 12:6 cf. 1:11; 9:7)**
>
> The son is loved by the owner and this reminds us of God's description of Jesus at his baptism and transfiguration. Jesus is seen by the disciples as the son who has come to collect that which is due to the owner.

4 What will be the owner's response? (Mark 12:9) What does Jesus want the religious authorities to see will happen?

He will punish. Their actions will be judged - they will be evicted from the vineyard and killed.

The vineyard will be 'given' to others, i.e. their privilege of being God's people will be taken from Israel and given to Jesus' disciples.

5 How should the religious authorities have responded to the parable? How did they? (Mark 12:12)

They should have seen themselves as tenants who have killed God's servants and now plotted to kill his son (Mk. 3:6). However, they now sought to arrest the son (Mk. 12:12), even though they seemed to know who Jesus was and had been warned about the consequences of rejecting him.

6 In what ways do we continue to rebel against God even though we have been warned?

This question is designed to help participants see the peril of continuing to reject Jesus.

ADDITIONAL NOTES FOR LEADERS

This study introduces themes from the Week 6 talk on 'Jesus - his resurrection'. The key point is that God will judge those who reject Jesus by failing to give him the necessary allegiance he deserves as God's son.

The vineyard was a common Old Testament symbol of Israel. In particular, this passage is very similar to Isaiah 5 where the people of Israel are rebuked for the terrible way in which they have rejected God and told of the rightness of God's coming judgement. Jesus' hearers would have understood that the 'man' in the parable was God, that the 'vineyard' was the people of God, and that the missing fruit was honour and allegiance to the Son.

OTHER POSSIBLE QUESTIONS

- What will God do to those who deny the authority of his Son?
- How is that clear from the parable?
- What is surprising about the reaction of the religious authorities?

You may choose to use these questions if you don't have time to discuss the whole study and just want to ask one or two key questions to draw out the main points of the passage.

CHRISTIANITY
EXPLORED

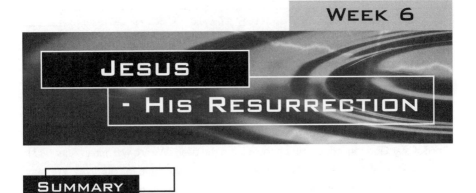

JESUS
- HIS RESURRECTION

SUMMARY

'He has risen!' (Mark 16:6)

Three days after Jesus' crucifixion some women went to the tomb where he was buried. On their journey they experience:

THE SHADOW OF DEATH

They have gone early in the morning to anoint the corpse of a murdered young man. They have watched Jesus' gruesome death and burial and must have been bewildered, heartbroken and drenched in sorrow. There is no doubt that Jesus is dead and the life they cared for has been murderously cut off in its prime.

THE SHOCK OF DISCOVERY

But when they get there they are stunned to find the stone rolled away, the body gone and the event explained by a divine messenger. He tells them, 'Don't be alarmed. You are looking for Jesus the Nazarene, who was crucified. He has risen! He is not here.' (Mark 16:6) Jesus had risen from the dead, just as he told them he would.

The resurrection of Jesus confirms everything that he said about himself – he really is God on earth; he really did come to earth to rescue rebels through his death on the cross; he really will come again to judge every person who ever lived.

THE SIGNIFICANCE FOR THE DISCIPLES

The words, 'He has risen!' change everything. They bring the Christian church into existence and provide us with a great hope and a great warning:

- **A great hope** because death is not the end. Christ has got through death himself and he can therefore get me through.

- **A great warning** because we will all be raised and judged. Jesus' resurrection is the proof that God can indeed raise people from the dead. We are warned in Acts 17:31 that we will all be raised to be judged and held accountable for our lives. We may like to think we are through with the past but the past is not through with us.

So what will **you** do with this great hope and this great warning?

THE BIG PICTURE OF MARK'S GOSPEL

Please read Mark 14:1 – 16:8

The following questions are designed to assist you in reading this passage. Note any questions you may have or anything you find of particular interest in the space provided at the back of this booklet. There will be time for these to be discussed next week.

Summary: Jesus goes willingly to his death on the cross and so fulfils God's purposes.

---

1 **To what extent is Jesus' death a mistake or accident and to what extent is it under Jesus' control?**
(Mark 10:33-34; 14:12-31, 48-49, 61-62)

Jesus predicted his death in detail and prepared for his death.

2 **To what extent is death easy for Jesus? (Mark 14:33-36; 15:34)**

Jesus' agony in the garden of Gethsemane and his cry of abandonment on the cross show just how hard his death was, as he bore God's anger at the world's rebellion.

Although he was separated from the Father, he bears it willingly.

CHRISTIANITY
EXPLORED

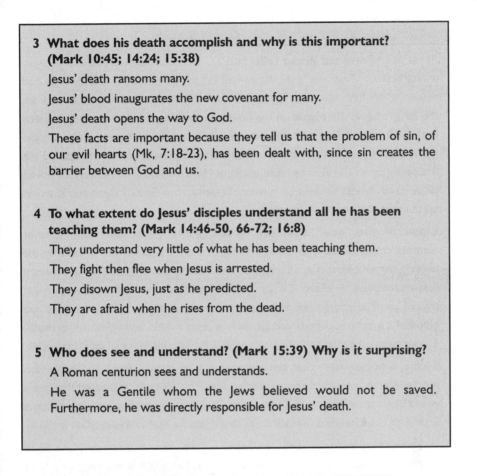

3 **What does his death accomplish and why is this important? (Mark 10:45; 14:24; 15:38)**

Jesus' death ransoms many.

Jesus' blood inaugurates the new covenant for many.

Jesus' death opens the way to God.

These facts are important because they tell us that the problem of sin, of our evil hearts (Mk, 7:18-23), has been dealt with, since sin creates the barrier between God and us.

4 **To what extent do Jesus' disciples understand all he has been teaching them? (Mark 14:46-50, 66-72; 16:8)**

They understand very little of what he has been teaching them.

They fight then flee when Jesus is arrested.

They disown Jesus, just as he predicted.

They are afraid when he rises from the dead.

5 **Who does see and understand? (Mark 15:39) Why is it surprising?**

A Roman centurion sees and understands.

He was a Gentile whom the Jews believed would not be saved. Furthermore, he was directly responsible for Jesus' death.

ADDITIONAL NOTES FOR LEADERS

MAIN POINTS OF THE PASSAGE

- Jesus dies to bring about the new covenant promised by the prophets (Mk. 14:24; cf. Jer. 31:23, 31-34) and to enable people to have free access to God (Mk. 15:37-39);

- Jesus dies innocently, willingly and in full control of events, yet at immense cost to himself;

- The disciples fail to understand, but we see God's ability to save even a Gentile soldier.

- **Feast of Unleavened Bread (Mk. 14:12)** - God commanded Israel to observe annual feasts of Passover and Unleavened Bread to remind them of how he had rescued them from slavery in Egypt (Ex. 12:14-20). Israel could only be saved from the tenth plague, the plague on the firstborn, by killing a lamb, eating its roasted flesh with bitter herbs and unleavened bread and smearing the blood on the doorpost. When God saw blood on a house, he passed over it and spared the firstborn (Ex. 12:1-13). The meal eaten in Mark 14:12-26 was clearly Passover. Jesus' death would be the true means of rescue from God's judgement; it would be the true Passover.

- **Blood of the 'new' covenant (Mk. 14:24)** - Not only did Passover commemorate rescue from slavery in Egypt and from the wrath of God by the pouring out of blood (Ex. 12:23), but that rescue was followed by a covenant that was ratified by blood (Ex. 24:6). The blood used to ratify a covenant was that of sacrifice and so the wine Jesus refers to in Mark 14:23-24 implies the blood of a substitute. The bread symbolises Jesus' whole body given up to death. The language of eating and drinking suggests the sharing in Jesus' sacrificial death.

  If 'new' is not intended then the meaning may be even wider: Jesus' death also satisfied the old covenant inaugurated at Sinai. This covenant stipulated that there would be curses as a result of disobedience. In dying on the cross, Jesus has become a curse for us and taken on himself the death penalty for man's rebellion (Gal. 3:10-13).

- **'Take this cup from me' (Mk. 14:36)** - For 'cup', see comment on Mark 10:38 (page 117). Jesus' anguish and obedience to his Father's will are seen clearly by this verse.

- **Was the darkness an eclipse? (Mk. 15:33)** - This idea is not possible as, at the time of the Passover, it is always a full moon. Therefore, earth would have been situated between the sun and the moon, (i.e. sun - earth - moon) rather than the moon being in the middle (sun - moon - earth), which is necessary for a daytime eclipse.

- **Why do we stop reading at Mark 16:8?** - Most scholars agree that Mark's Gospel ends at chapter 16, verse 8. The women flee still partially blind, like Peter, who had himself just denied Christ three times (Mk. 14:66-72). The ending provokes the question: Have you yet seen who Jesus is, why he came, and what it means to follow him? Verses 9-19 appear to be attempts by later writers to add a fuller resurrection ending to Mark. However, the oldest manuscripts do not include this section and its style and vocabulary are different from the rest of Mark.

CHRISTIANITY
EXPLORED

FOCUS IN

In our time next week we will be looking in more detail at Mark 14:1–11. You may find it helpful to think about the following questions in advance of the session.

1 **What do we learn about the opposition to Jesus from this passage? In what way is it surprising? (Mark 14:1-2, 10-11)**

Jesus is opposed by the religious leaders, just as he predicted (Mk. 14:1-2 cf. 8:31).

However, Jesus is also opposed by Judas, who is one of the twelve apostles (Mk. 14:10-11).

2 **How does Mark highlight the woman's response to Jesus? In what ways is it an appropriate response? (Mark 14:4-8, cf. 10:13-15; 12:41-44)**

Jesus rebukes some of those present for their indignation - they are like the unwelcoming disciples back in Mark 10:13-15.

The woman did what she could and gave what she had - she is like the widow in Mark 12:41-44. Jesus wants the disciples to know that she displayed the right response to Jesus.

3 **How does Jesus interpret her actions? (Mark 14:8)**

He accepts it as preparation for his burial: his death is certain and imminent.

4 **Complete the table below to sum up the different responses to Jesus. Who do you think responded in the right way?**

PEOPLE	RESPONSES TO JESUS
Religious leaders	They plot to arrest and kill Jesus.
Some other people present	They are indignant at the woman's response because they see it as wasteful. They are unwelcoming (Mk. 10:13-15), even though they appear to follow Jesus' teaching (Mk. 14:5; cf. 10:21).
Woman	She prepares for Jesus' death. She does what she can - her priority is to make a right response to Jesus' imminent death.
Judas	He betrays Jesus and looks for an opportunity to hand Jesus over. He takes money for his betrayal.

5 With which of the four groups do you identify? How should you respond to Jesus?

This question is designed to enable participants to see how responses which may appear OK are actually denials of Christ.

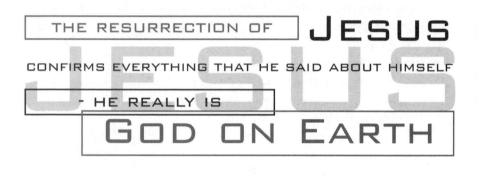

THE RESURRECTION OF **JESUS**

CONFIRMS EVERYTHING THAT HE SAID ABOUT HIMSELF

- HE REALLY IS

GOD ON EARTH

ADDITIONAL NOTES FOR LEADERS

This study deals with the need to respond rightly to Jesus and thus introduces themes from the Week 7 talk on 'What is a Christian?' Mark places the story of the anointing (Mk. 14:3-9) between the opposition from the religious authorities (Mk. 14:1-2) and the opposition from one of the 12 disciples (Mk. 14:10-11) to enable us to contrast the woman's attitude with that of the religious authorities and Judas. Indeed, she is also contrasted with 'some of those present' (Mk. 14:4).

OTHER POSSIBLE QUESTIONS

- How do some of the people present view the woman's actions? Why?
- How does Jesus view her actions? Why?
- How does she differ from the religious leaders and Judas?

You may choose to use these questions if you don't have time to discuss the whole study and just want to ask one or two key questions to draw out the main points of the passage.

CHRISTIANITY
E✝PLORED

Before anyone is asked to make a commitment to follow Jesus Christ it is important that they understand what the Christian life is like – and that is the theme of the Weekend Away.

The opening talk, based on the teaching of the Apostle Peter (who was Mark's primary source on Jesus Christ) informs us that the Christian life is tough. But that does not mean that we don't have the resources to live it. Indeed we're given:

| 1 THE CHURCH FAMILY; |
| 2 THE HOLY SPIRIT; |
| 3 PRAYER; |
| 4 THE BIBLE; |

to help us live for Christ.

YOU'RE ☐ NEVER ALONE

YOU'RE NEVER ALONE
- THE CHURCH FAMILY

SUMMARY

1 Peter 1:1-8

As we ask, 'What is the Christian life like?' we see that it is tough, but we are never alone because we have the church family.

When facing trials we need to remember:

• we have been chosen by God (v. 1);
• we have a living hope for the future (v. 3);
• God calls us to 'love one another deeply, from the heart' (v. 22).

If you are right at the start of the Christian life you mustn't think you can do this alone. You've got to be pro-active and build a team of wise people around you who will help you to follow Christ: 'He who walks with the wise grows wise, but a companion of fools suffers harm.' (Proverbs 13:20)

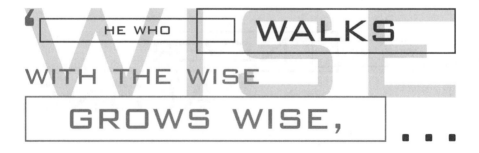

HE WHO WALKS WITH THE WISE GROWS WISE, ■ ■ ■

CHRISTIANITY
EXPLORED

YOU'RE NEVER ALONE
- THE HOLY SPIRIT

SUMMARY

John 16.

The essence of the Christian life is not **distance** but **presence**: the close, personal indwelling presence of the Holy Spirit in my life now, drawing me to Christ and causing Christ to grow in my heart.

He opens our eyes to see our desperate state before God and our need of his mercy, given to us through Christ's death.

The moment we accept Christ as our Master and Saviour we will be joined by an expert who reveals Christ in a way that strengthens, encourages and blesses us because he brings all the power and resources of the Lord Jesus to bear upon our situation. The Holy Spirit universalises and internalises the presence of Jesus by:

• illumining our mind as we read the Bible;
• gifting every Christian to play a unique role in God's church;
• convicting us of sin in our lives and
• bringing lasting peace to our hearts.

BUT

A COMPANION OF

FOOLS

SUFFERS HARM'

PROVERBS 13:20

YOU'RE NEVER ALONE
- THE HOLY SPIRIT

John 14:15–27

Just before Jesus is arrested and then crucified, he promises the disciples that, once he has gone, he will send the Holy Spirit to be with them.

Read John chapter 14, verses 15–27. Write down any words or phrases you are not sure of and would like to ask about in the space provided at the back of this booklet.

1 **Why does Jesus call the Spirit another Counsellor? (v. 16)**

The word for another here means 'just the same as'. A mother might ask a child who has dropped their ice-cream, 'Do you want another one, **just the same** as the one you dropped?' So the Holy Spirit is another Counsellor, just the same as Jesus. The Holy Spirit is therefore God.

2 **Why does Jesus refer to the Holy Spirit as 'him'? (v. 17)**

He is a person to be respected, not a force or an energy to be manipulated. He is the one through whom we have relationship with the Father and the Son (v. 23); he is not an 'it'.

3 **What can we learn from the titles given to the Holy Spirit?**

'Another Counsellor' (v.16) - the literal meaning of the term counsellor is 'one who comes alongside'. This is a great reassurance to Christians facing temptation, doubt, demanding service or opposition. We are not alone. Christ is alongside us through his Holy Spirit.

'Spirit of Truth' (v.17) - the apostles were reassured in verse 26 that the Holy Spirit would enable them to remember Christ's teachings and lead them into all truth. As we read the Bible we can be very thankful for its trustworthy, divine authorship.

4 What does Jesus promise he will not do and why is this so significant at this point? (v. 18)

Jesus promises not to leave his disciples as orphans. This is significant because they are about to see him killed (v. 19). The other great religious leaders, such as Buddha and Mohammed, have gone; they have left their followers. Jesus does not abandon his people because he gives them the Holy Spirit. Jesus says, 'I will come to you.'

5 What does Jesus promise he will do? (v. 18) What, therefore, is central to the Holy Spirit's ministry? (See also John 16:14)

Jesus promises to take up residence in the lives of his followers. He universalises and internalises his presence with each Christian believer. 'He lives with you and will be in you.' The Spirit makes Jesus real to us.

6 If I have a close relationship with God the Father and the Lord Jesus through the Holy Spirit living in me, what is the sign of that? (vv. 23-24)

This is shown by obedience to Jesus' teaching - love is shown by actions, not just by emotion. The way I show I love somebody is by the way I act towards them. The name Holy Spirit conveys the Spirit's holiness and his opposition to sin. When we disobey Christ we grieve the Holy Spirit.

7 What is the world's response to this teaching about the Holy Spirit? (v. 17)

The world cannot respond or relate to him because it doesn't see or know him.

THE ESSENCE OF THE

CHRISTIAN LIFE

IS NOT DISTANCE

BUT PRESENCE

SUMMARY

Acts 4: 23–31

Prayer is important because of:
- who we pray to;
- who we pray through;
- how we pray.

We pray to the Sovereign Lord - the supreme ruler who made the heaven and the earth and everything in them. This God, the creator of the universe, also values me so much that he allows me to call him 'Daddy'.

We pray through the Son. He has reconciled me to God through the cross and my prayer life gains access to the Father because the Son has removed my sin.

When we come to the Sovereign Lord, our Father, we pour out our heart. At its root, prayer is a friendship with God. He speaks to us in the Bible and we speak to him in prayer. And as we go through life we develop this friendship with God but, like any friendship, it depends on being honest, being natural and speaking regularly.

Above all, we have to trust that God is in control. When we pray and ask God for things, we may not get the answer we want - and that can be very hard because sometimes we may not understand God's plan until we see the Lord Jesus face to face in heaven.

It is useful to question the motive behind your requests. If God answered your prayer your way:

- Would it bring glory to him?
- Would it benefit his kingdom - that is, would it be good for his purposes?
- Would it help other people?
- Would it help you to grow to know God better?

CHRISTIANITY
EXPLORED

SUMMARY

Psalm 1 shows us:

- We are not to be influenced by the people who live without reference to God (v. 1).

- We are to delight in the law of the Lord (v. 2). This shapes our thinking and life as we meditate on it, pore over it, bring life to bear on it.

- If we stay close to the Lord Jesus Christ we will draw constant nourishment and spiritual vitality (v. 3).

- We are faced with the choice of being like a living tree or dead straw and our destinies are determined by our choices (vv. 4–6).

WHO IS IT WRITTEN BY?

'All Scripture is God-breathed' (2 Timothy 3:14–17). The Bible was written 100% by human beings, but it was also 100% inspired by God.

WHAT IS IT ABOUT?

The Bible is about salvation – how to get right with God through Jesus. The start of the book describes how God made the world and meant for us to live in relationship with him. We turned our back on him, but God didn't turn his back on us and ultimately he sent his Son to die so that we could be forgiven our sins and brought back into relationship with him. Then Christ rose again – so the resurrection promises us eternal life – and we're promised that Christ will return.

WHAT IS IT FOR?

Its purpose is for me to be able to live a godly life (2 Timothy 3:16-17). It teaches me how to live – what is right and wrong and which way to go. When I'm faced with big decisions I go to this book. I talk to Christian friends and ask, 'How does the Bible guide me on this so that I can make a godly decision?' And then I ask God to help me make that decision.

HOW DO WE MAKE TIME TO READ IT?

Reading the Bible is all about making choices. Deciding how you use your time is about making choices. Consider the example of Martha in Luke 10:38–42. If you are too busy to read your Bible and pray, then you're too busy.

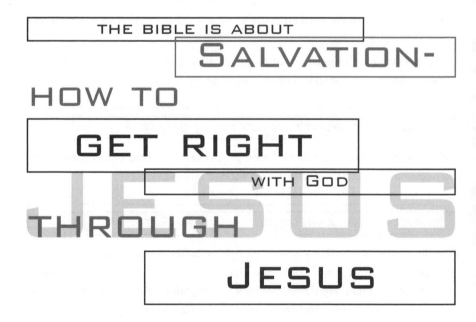

THE BIBLE IS ABOUT

SALVATION-

HOW TO

GET RIGHT

WITH GOD

THROUGH JESUS

JESUS

CHRISTIANITY
EXPLORED

THE MOTIVATION
TO KEEP GOING

Ephesians 2:1–10

Read Ephesians chapter 2, verses 1–10 to see the verses in their context. Write down any words and phrases you are not sure of and would like to ask about in the space provided at the back of this booklet.

The numbered questions can be answered directly from the passage. The **'Think it Through'** questions help you to reflect in more depth what it means.

---

1 **Write out Ephesians chapter 2 verses 8-9 in your own words.**

2 **What has happened to the Christian by grace and how is that clear from the rest of the passage?**

   The Christian has been made alive with Christ and saved (vv. 5,8). The Christian has been raised up and seated with Christ (v. 6).

3 **What is the appropriate response to God's grace, i.e. to God's gift of salvation?**

   To show gratitude for the gift (v. 8); not to boast (v. 9); to do good works (v. 10).

From what has the Christian been saved?

The Christian has been saved from death (v. 1), from personal sin (v. 1), from the power of the devil (v. 2) and from God's wrath (v. 3).

How has the Christian been saved?

'It is by grace that you have been saved.' (v. 8) We have been saved because of God's great love for us (v. 4) and we then have faith in the gift of grace (v. 8).

Faith involves more than knowing about God. What else is involved?

Faith involves reliance on God's love for us, which has made us alive with Christ and saved us (v. 5).

Have you responded to Jesus in faith?

This question is designed to help the participants work out where they stand in relation to God's grace.

4 Is salvation my own work?

Salvation is entirely from God: 'Not by works, so that no-one can boast' (v. 9).

5 In what way does salvation come to us from God?

It is a gift which we receive (v. 8).

6 What can I contribute to my salvation?

Nothing - the only thing which we bring is our sin! (v. 1).

7 What credit can I get for my salvation?

None - God gets the credit because of his great love (v. 4), mercy (v. 4) and kindness (v. 7).

What have I learned about salvation as a result of this study?

Hopefully the participants will have learned that they are more wicked than they ever realised (vv.1-3) but more loved than they ever dreamed (vv. 4-10). They will see that salvation is a result of God's grace (v. 8) and his great love (v. 4).

How does this affect my understanding about who receives salvation?

The people who receive salvation are those who realise they need to be rescued from the state that is described in verses 1-3.

Is there any attitude I should change, or action I should take?

This question is designed to highlight whether we see ourselves in the condition described in verses 1-3 or as people who have just spiritually lapsed a little?

How good do I have to be in order to be saved?

There may be those who have always thought that you trust in good works in order to be accepted by God. They believe they are accepted by being good enough, giving to charity, not lying, being a good citizen, going to church, praying, getting confirmed, or whatever. Can they see that they are more wicked than they ever realised and that they can never earn their salvation?

What good works have I done to earn my salvation?

It may be helpful for individuals in the group to explain what they are trusting in to get them accepted by God.

Who can the Christian thank for their salvation?

God alone, as he gives us the gift of grace through Jesus Christ.

Other Bible passages to look at:
- John 3:16-17
- John 1:9-13
- Titus 3: 4-7

- Grace - unmerited favour; generosity.
- Faith - the attitude of reliance, trust, dependence. In Ephesians chapter 2 this refers to trusting in the death of Christ.

Adapted from *Just for Starters* © St Matthias Press, 1992
Just for Starters published by Matthias Media/The Good Book Company

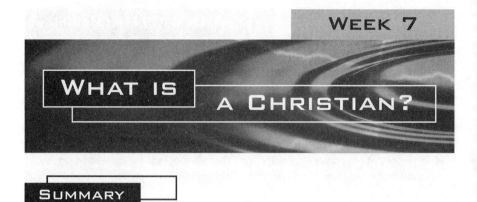

WHAT IS A CHRISTIAN?

SUMMARY

Mark 8: 27–38

A Christian is somebody who not only knows the answers to the following three questions, but also acts upon those answers.

1 WHO IS JESUS?

(MARK 8:27-30)

This is the half-way point in Mark's Gospel and Peter, the other disciples and the reader are all asked this scorching, personal question by Jesus: 'Who do you say I am?' Peter, with his answer, 'You are the Christ', has at last seen – after all the evidence of Mark chapters 1–8 – that Jesus is not just a man. No, he is in fact the Christ, God's king. A Christian is somebody who has seen that Jesus is God's king.

So what about you? Can you only see the human face of Jesus or can you see the divine face as well?

2 WHY DID JESUS COME?

(MARK 8:31-33)

A new section of the gospel now begins: the reader must not only see that Jesus is God's king, but also the type of king he is - that he is a king who came to suffer and die so that he could rescue mankind from the judgement we deserve. Just as we may only see Jesus as a man, so we may only see the cross as a tragic, politically-motivated murder. That is all Peter can see at this point, as he rebukes Jesus and tells

CHRISTIANITY
EXPLORED

him not to go to the cross. Peter thinks that Jesus, as God's king, belongs on a throne, not a cross. He cannot see that Jesus' throne **is** his cross.

So what about you? How do you understand the cross? What do you believe happened there? Do you believe that Jesus died to rescue you from **hell**, through the **cross**, for **heaven**?

3 WHAT DOES JESUS DEMAND?

(MARK 8:34–38)

Jesus calls anyone who wants to be one of his people to turn away from their allegiance to themselves and instead to follow him. He is saying that a true Christian is no longer going to live for themselves but for him (Mark 8:34). If we commit ourselves to Christ then discipleship could mean martyrdom, to the extent of being nailed to a cruel cross and dying in agony. So this is Jesus' offer to his hearers: I will die for you, but you must take up your cross if you want to follow me.' It's a cross for a cross; it's a call to come and die. At the very least it's a call to die to the right to run my life my way.

But is this a suicide gesture? No, because Jesus gives us a convincing reason to follow him (Mark 8:35–37). He is trying to teach us some perspective here, for there are two different time frames which we need to keep in mind. By nature, we tend to focus on our present circumstances and in this instant culture if something doesn't pay now then people are not very interested. Jesus lifts our eyes from the present and reminds us of the future; he teaches us that there is a connection between the choices we make now and the future that awaits us. We all have souls - **that** part of us, indeed the heart of us, that lives forever. Jesus is saying, 'Don't waste your soul; you can never buy it back. In the long-term, if you bring me your life, energy, resources, heart, mind and love, you will save your life and your soul.'

There are three basic questions which any thinking person will always ask about the Christian faith before becoming a Christian. It may be that you are now in a position to answer these three questions:

• Question 1: Who is Jesus? *Answer: You are the Christ.*

• Question 2: Why did Jesus come? *Answer: To die for me; so that I can be forgiven.*

• Question 3: What does Jesus demand? *Answer: That I die to the right to run my life my way and choose to obey Jesus instead.*

These three answers are summed up in the following prayer. If you want to become a Christian then this would be an appropriate prayer to pray.

'Lord Jesus, I recognise that you are God and have the right to control my life. I have rebelled against you, sinning in my thoughts, my words and my actions; sometimes unconsciously, sometimes deliberately. I am sorry for the way I have lived and ask you to forgive me. As best I can, I want to turn away from rebellion and obey you. Thank you, Lord Jesus, for dying for me on the cross. Please come into my life and take complete control of it. Amen.'

If you have prayed this prayer here are some great encouragements for you from Mark's Gospel.

1 The Holy Spirit (Mark 1:8)
Jesus Christ comes to live in you by his Spirit and now begins to change you from the inside out.

2 The forgiveness of sins (Mark 2:10)
You can know for certain that your sins are totally forgiven because Jesus' death was sufficient to pay for your sins.

3 Eternal life (Mark 10:29-30)
You can know for certain that you have eternal life and can trust in what Jesus has done, rather than in what you can do.

AM I A CHRISTIAN?

Test yourself - you are a Christian if you can genuinely say yes to the following statements:

- I trust in Jesus' death for the forgiveness of my sins - I do not trust my own good works.

- I trust in the risen Jesus to be Lord of my life - I will not insist solely on my own will.

CHRISTIANITY
EXPLORED

THE DEVIL & ASSURANCE

SUMMARY

Ephesians 6:10–18

The Bible teaches us that there are powerful, complex and intelligent forces that are out to destroy every Christian: we are involved in an unseen spiritual battle.

The devil is called the father of lies (John 8:44), but there are three great truths which unshakingly support our relationship with God:

- **The cross of Christ** reminds us that **forgiveness is a gift that Christ has fully paid for**. We are accepted by God - not because we deserve it or have done enough, but because we have trusted in what Christ has done for us. Jesus said on the cross: 'Tetelesti - it is finished. Your past, present and future sin is all forgiven. I've paid off all your debts.'

- **The word of the Father** is totally reliable and assures us that we are not alone. In times of anxiety, indecision, loneliness or temptation we can trust God's promises in the Bible.

- **The witness of the Holy Spirit** makes us aware of an inner battle and reassures us that God is at work in our lives. The presence of the Holy Spirit gives a deep peace that passes understanding (Philippians 4:7) and reminds us that we are God's children; yet the same Holy Spirit is also still at work transforming us from within and forcing us to battle daily against our sinful natures.

FORGIVENESS IS A GIFT THAT CHRIST HAS FULLY PAID FOR

COLOSSIANS 1:21-23A

The following Bible study relates to this week's talk and is designed for leaders to go through with course participants after the talk.

Please read Colossians chapter 1 verses 21–23a. Write down any words, phrases or verses that you do not understand in the space provided at the back of this booklet. Please also read Ephesians 2:1–10, which is a helpful parallel passage.

BEFORE WE TRUST CHRIST ... (VERSE 21)

1 What state is described in verse 21?

Enemies in your minds.

2 What do you think it means to be 'alienated from God'?

It means to be cut off, exiled, banished; not in a relationship with him.

3 Where does this alienation originate and how does it show itself?

It originates in the mind and shows itself in evil behaviour. Compare Romans 1:18 where the rebellion begins with the suppression of truth and works itself out in godless and wicked behaviour.

THINK IT THROUGH

To whom do you think this description applies? (See Ephesians 2:1-3)

The keys words here are 'as for you' (v. 1) and 'all of us' (v. 3).

How do you feel about this description of mankind?

This question should encourage participants to grasp the truth of being more wicked than we ever realised.

CHRISTIANITY
EXPLORED

4 Who is the 'he' in verse 22? What has he achieved and how?

God is the subject of this verse. He has reconciled us through Christ's death on the cross.

5 What is the significance of the tense?

It is in the past tense, indicating that it has already taken place. I have been reconciled to God if I trust in what Christ has done. There is nothing more that has to be done.

6 In whose eyes can we be 'without blemish and free from accusation' and why is this important?

We can be like this in God's eyes. It is important because we are guilty (v. 21); we were God's enemies and behaved in an evil way, and yet we can now be free from accusation. This means that we are like condemned men and women who receive a pardon.

THINK IT THROUGH

Who has done the reconciling in verse 22 and what is the significance of this?

God has done the reconciling and it is his work alone.

What do we need to do in order to achieve our salvation?

We can do nothing. We just trust in what Christ has done and receive the gift of forgiveness (Eph. 2:8-9).

How can this act as an assurance for us when we do not feel worthy of being a Christian?

Once we have trusted in what Christ has done, how we feel is then irrelevant. Sometimes our feelings may not testify to the truth that we are accepted by God.

7 What is the proviso in verse 23a?

The proviso is that we continue in our faith.

8 Why is it so important ?

There is only one place where we are promised that we can be free from accusation - that place is the cross. If we move away from trusting in the cross then we are once more alienated from God. This is where God has provided forgiveness; it is through Jesus' death that we will be presented without blemish and free from accusation (v. 22).

9 How can we remain 'established and firm'?

We must keep going back to Christ and trusting in him. He is supreme (Col. 1:15-20). We must continue to live in him (Col. 2:6-7).

THINK IT THROUGH

Do you have issues and struggles which cause you to feel doubt about the gospel?

In the book of Colossians the false teachers were drawing people away from Christ by saying that they needed more than Christ. They claimed, for example, that people could find a greater fullness in various rituals or experiences.

What should you do?

Remember Christ has reconciled you to God (Col. 1:22) and therefore keep overflowing with thankfulness (Col. 1:12; 2:7; 3:15; 4:2). The theme of thankfulness for what Christ has done resonates through this book.

Highlight a verse from this study which you would find helpful to remember when you feel doubt. Try to learn it and use it when you need to.

CHRISTIANITY
E_XPLORED

WEEK 9

CHOICES — KING HEROD

SUMMARY

Mark 6: 14–29

We all need to make choices - and face the consequences of our decisions. As Meryl Streep says in *The Bridges of Madison County*, '**We are the choices that we have made.**'

Herod made two key choices:

• He chose to rebel – he knew he was living without reference to the God who made him.

• He chose not to repent – he was not prepared to turn from his rebellion and seek the forgiveness God offered.

Like Herod, many people today will deny what they know is right when they find themselves in the valley of decision, afraid of what family, colleagues or friends will think.

Mark is asking all of us, 'What choices are you going to make?'

It's an important question: while we are free to choose whether or not to repent, we are not free to determine the consequences of our choice.

WE ARE THE CHOICES THAT WE HAVE MADE

MARK 9:30-50

The following Bible study relates to this week's talk and is designed for leaders to go through with course participants after the talk.

Context: In Mark 8:31 – 9:29 Jesus has made it clear that he must suffer and die and that his followers must be prepared to lose their lives for Jesus and the gospel. The cost of not being a Christian is far higher, since Jesus will return to judge those who are ashamed of him and his words. However, the disciples fail to understand why Jesus must die.

Please read Mark 9:30–50. Write down any words, phrases or verses that you do not understand in the space provided at the back of this booklet.

1 **Why is the disciples' conversation so shocking? (Mark 9:33-34 cf. 9:31; 8:34-38)**

They are concerned with greatness when Jesus has been talking about his need to be killed. They have already been told that followers of Jesus must deny themselves and be willing to lose their lives in this world.

2 **How does Jesus explain and illustrate what true greatness is like? (Mark 9:35-37).**

Jesus tells them that true greatness looks like being last and serving all.

Jesus takes a child and calls on them to 'welcome' children as an example of serving.

They are to do so in Jesus' name, i.e. do as Jesus would do. By dying on the cross, Jesus would become 'little' to welcome and serve all.

3 **What had the disciples done, according to John's words in Mark 9:38? Why was this wrong? (Mark 9:39-40).**

They had prevented someone else from casting out demons.

They were not doing what Jesus called them to do in Mark 9:35-37, i.e. they were not welcoming others in Jesus' name.

4 How should Christians behave towards one another? (Mark 9:41)

Christians should serve one another and, in doing so, they will not lose their reward.

5 How should Christians *not* behave towards one another? (Mark 9:42)

Christians should not cause one another to sin. This passage communicates the need to be ruthless with those things that could lead us into sin. They must be cut out.

6 Why is this so serious? (Mark 9:42-50)

Because sin leads to hell and hell is an awful place.

Hell is so awful we would do anything to avoid going there.

7 Where, given Mark 9:38, does that leave Jesus' disciples and us? (Also Mark 7:18-23)

Mark 9:38 helps us to see that the disciples were doing the opposite of what Jesus commanded them earlier when he gave them authority over evil spirits and power to heal (Mk. 6:6-13). Their enthusiasm to stop someone else driving out demons could be seen as causing that person to sin. They were therefore heading for hell (Mk 9:43-47), unable to do anything about it. We have already seen in Mark 7:18-23 that our problem is not our hand or foot or eye - but our evil hearts. We are therefore also in need of heart surgery and rescue from hell.

8 How then, should we respond through what we have learned:

To God? (cf. Mark 9:24)

We should cry for help and rescue.

To one another? (cf. Mark 9:50)

We should see ourselves as deserving only hell and therefore stop arguing about who is the greatest but rather be at peace with one another.

We should serve one another rather than causing one another to sin.

9 What choices do you need to make as a result of what you have learned?

This question is designed for personal reflection on both the Herod talk and this Bible study.

CHOICES - JAMES & JOHN

SUMMARY

Mark 10: 32–52

In this passage the choices different people make could not be presented more starkly:

• The disciples chose glory – James and John sought power and prestige.

• Jesus chose service – he willingly accepted pain and humiliation instead of honour.

• Bartimaeus chose mercy – he recognised that he deserved nothing from Jesus, but asked him to show kindness which was totally undeserved.

James and John were self-satisfied and self-seeking and as a result they saw no need for Jesus to die. But Jesus went to the cross, dying to pay the ransom price to rescue many.

How should we respond to Jesus? If we have already trusted him for our forgiveness we need to learn that following Jesus is about service not status. If we have not put our trust in him, we need to cry out to him for mercy.

BIBLE STUDY

MARK 10:32-52

The following Bible study relates to this week's talk and is designed for leaders to go through with course participants after the talk.

Context: From Mark 8:31 onwards, Jesus has taught that he must suffer and die. Jesus has also taught that his followers must choose to follow the way of the cross in serving others and in being last not first, instead of causing others to sin, which leads to hell. Hell is so awful that, if we could, we would do anything to avoid going

CHRISTIANITY
EXPLORED

there. However, we are helpless to do anything about our human hearts and salvation is possible only with God (Mark 10:27).

Please read Mark 10:32–52. Write down any words, phrases or verses that you do not understand in the space provided at the back of this booklet.

---

1 Given last week's study and Mark 10:32-34, what is wrong with what James and John are seeking in Mark 10:35-41?

They want glory and have not yet seen that greatness comes only by serving - the clearest example of which is Jesus going to the cross.

2 How does Jesus answer them in Mark 10:38 and 41-44? What is the model to follow? (Mark 10:45)

Jesus says that they don't know what they're talking about; they can't drink God's cup of wrath - only Jesus can.

Jesus reminds them that his followers are servants who go the way of the cross.

3 How is Bartimaeus contrasted with James and John? (Mark 10:46-52 cf. 10:35-41)

They have different titles for Jesus and different requests - they want glory, he wants mercy.

4 How does Jesus react to him and why is that important? (Mark 10:49-52)

Jesus calls Bartimaeus and heals him.

A miracle is required to see why Jesus has come.

5 In what ways are we tempted to behave like James and John?

For example, by desiring status and power rather than seeking to serve.

6 When tempted, what do we need to remember?

That Jesus, the glorious Son of Man, had to suffer and die in this world to ransom many.

---

7 What does the incident with Bartimaeus tell us about how to be saved?

We are to recognise who Jesus is and cry to him for mercy.

8 What choices do you need to make in the light of all that you have learned on *Christianity Explored*?

You will remember that at the end of week 7 we gave all those that came an opportunity to follow Christ and trust in what he has done for them. The biblical words for this are to repent and believe. Having had three more weeks of exposure to Mark's Gospel it may be that you now want to echo in your heart the prayer that you first heard three weeks ago.

'Lord Jesus, I recognise that you are God and have the right to control my life. I have rebelled against you, sinning in my thoughts, my words and my actions; sometimes unconsciously, sometimes deliberately. I am sorry for the way I have lived and ask you to forgive me. As best I can, I want to turn away from rebellion and obey you. Thank you, Lord Jesus, for dying for me on the cross. Please come into my life and take complete control of it. Amen.'

WHAT'S YOUR EVANGELISM STYLE?

Each of the six evangelism styles makes a unique contribution to the process of leading people to Christ. A brief outline of characteristics is given here to help you identify your style or styles of evangelism. You can then look for specific opportunities and events to use your style most effectively and play to your strengths.

CONFRONTATIONAL
(E.G PETER IN ACTS 2:1-39)

- Confident
- Bold
- Direct
- Skips small talk; gets right to the point
- Has strong opinions and convictions

INTELLECTUAL
(E.G. PAUL IN ACTS 17:16-31)

- Analytical
- Logical
- Inquisitive
- Likes to debate ideas
- More concerned with what people think than what they feel

THE APPENDICES

TESTIMONIAL

(E.G THE BLIND MAN IN JOHN 9:1-34)

- Clear communicator
- Good listener
- Vulnerable to ups and downs of personal life
- Overwhelmed by the account of how God reached them
- Sees links between their own experience and others

INTERPERSONAL

(E.G. MATTHEW IN LUKE 5:29)

- Conversational
- Compassionate
- Sensitive
- Friendship-oriented
- Focuses on people and their needs

INVITATIONAL

(E.G. THE WOMAN AT THE WELL,

IN JOHN 4:28-30)

- Hospitable
- Persuasive
- Enjoys meeting new people
- Committed to things they believe in
- Sees outreach events as unique opportunities

CHRISTIANITY
EXPLORED

SERVING

(E.G. DORCAS IN ACTS 9:36)

- Patient
- Others-centred
- Sees needs and finds joy in meeting them
- Shows love through action more than words
- Attaches value to even menial tasks

Adapted from *Becoming a Contagious Christian: Participant's Guide*, by Mark Mittelberg © Willow Creek Association. Used by permission. This guide is part of a training course which includes a more complete questionnaire that can help you further identify your evangelism style as well as give you practical steps for developing that style. More information on the *Becoming a Contagious Christian* evangelism course is available by calling 0044 (0)845 1300 909.

THE RELIABILITY
OF THE GOSPELS

APPENDIX II

Some enquirers come to *Christianity Explored* believing the Bible is a book of myths. The table on page 161 is a useful tool to overcome this, by establishing the historical reliability of the Gospels. For some, filling in this chart has enabled them to read Mark's Gospel with much greater confidence.

If this issue comes up during a group discussion time, the leaders are asked to give out copies of the chart with the Gospel information missing (available in *The Handbook*). The participants are then asked to fill in the blanks, bearing in mind the comparisons with the other historical writings.

The leaders should have the answers from the completed chart to hand to facilitate the discussion.

ARE THE GOSPELS ACCURATE RECORDS?

If the originals do not exist, then the procedure for assessing the reliability of records is as follows:

1 How many copies have been found? (and how similar are they?)

2 How old are these copies - what is the time lag between the original document and the copies which now exist?

Ancient Writing	Thucydides History	Caesar's Gallic War	Tacitus' History	The Four Gospels
Date of original document 'A'	460 - 400 BC	58-50 BC	AD 100	AD 42 - 90
Oldest surviving copy 'B'	AD 900 plus a few 1st century fragments	AD 850	AD 800	Earliest copy of Mark's Gospel - AD 130 Earliest New Testament - AD 350
Approximate time between 'A' and 'B'	1,300 years	900 years	700 years	200 years
Number of ancient copies in existence today	8	10	2	5,000 Greek 10,000 Latin 9,300 others

Is the Bible Historically Reliable or a Book of Stories?

What the ancient historians say:

1 Pliny (AD 112)   civil servant of Emperor Trajan speaks at length about the activities of the early Christians;

2 Tacitus   (contemporary of Pliny) describes early Christians;

3 Thallus (AD 52)   a Samaritan historian discusses the darkness that fell during the crucifixion that is recorded in Luke 23: 44-45;

4 Josephus (AD 70)   mentions Pilate, Annas, Caiaphas, the Herods, Felix, Festus, John the Baptist and Jesus, who he calls a, 'doer of marvellous deeds' and 'condemned to the cross'.

Josephus, *Antiquities xviii* state:

> About this time arose Jesus, a wise man, if indeed it be lawful to call him a man. For he was a doer of wonderful deeds, and a teacher of men who gladly receive the truth. He drew to himself many both of the Jews and of the Gentiles. He was the Christ; and when Pilate, on the indictment of the principal men among us, had condemned him to the cross, those who had loved him at first did not cease to do so, for he appeared to them again alive on the third day, the divine prophets having foretold these and ten thousand other wonderful things about him. And even to this day the race of Christians, who are named from him, has not died out.

WHAT ARCHAEOLOGISTS HAVE FOUND:

- Many digs have verified the Gospel accounts, e.g. the pool of Bethesda and five colonnades (John 5:1-2);

- Tombs sealed in AD 50 with the inscription inside: 'Jesus let him arise'.

CHRISTIANITY
EXPLORED